I Call Him
"Mr. President"

To Art,
   As "41" lived.
~~Family~~. Faith, and Friends.
     Honored to share -
      Please Enjoy!
        Ken Raynor

I Call Him "Mr. President"

Stories of Golf, Fishing, and Life with My Friend

George H. W. Bush

KEN RAYNOR
with **MICHAEL PATRICK SHIELS**

Foreword by **BARBARA BUSH**

Skyhorse Publishing

Skyhorse Publishing books may be purchased in bulk at special discounts for sales promotion, corporate gifts, fund-raising, or educational purposes. Special editions can also be created to specifications. For details, contact the Special Sales Department, Skyhorse Publishing, 307 West 36th Street, 11th Floor, New York, NY 10018 or info@skyhorsepublishing.com.

Skyhorse® and Skyhorse Publishing® are registered trademarks of Skyhorse Publishing, Inc.®, a Delaware corporation.

Visit our website at www.skyhorsepublishing.com.

10 9 8 7 6 5 4 3 2

Library of Congress Cataloging-in-Publication Data is available on file.

Cover design by Brian Peterson
Front cover photo credit White House photo/David Valdez
Back cover photo credit White House photo/Susan Biddle

ISBN: 978-1-5107-2464-8
Ebook ISBN: 978-1-5107-2465-5

Printed in the United States of America

Note: Author Ken Raynor's proceeds from the sale of this book will be donated to the Kennebunkport Conservation Trust and Portland Mercy Hospital's "Gary's House" via the Gary Pike George H. W. Bush Cape Arundel Golf Classic.

To the people who already know the details without reading this story cover to cover: my wife Anne and son Kyle. Together, side by side, we have experienced nights at the White House, eighteen holes, or simple, quiet dinners at the Raynors' or Bushes' homes. It's this bond and love that our families share that have made these experiences so special. Simply, we did it together!

Contents

Foreword

By Barbara Bush

When our dear friend Ken asked me to write this foreword — for a book about fishing and golf, of all things — to be perfectly honest I thought he had lost his mind. After all, I know absolutely nothing about fishing . . . except that it usually takes a long time.

And as for golf, I think I maybe shot under 100 one time, and that was thanks to Ken's patient tutoring. So no expertise there either.

But then I realized something. This is really *not* a book about golf and fishing so much as it is, for George and me at least, a story about friendship.

It's about two men who love being out on the water, even in the roughest of seas, if the fish are biting — and even when they are not.

It's about two men who love to battle it out on the course, even in a driving rainstorm.

And it's about two men who love Maine, and their families, and their legions of friends.

Put in that light, I am happy for Ken — and for you as the reader — because he truly has been a good friend during a remarkable period of George's life. The time they spent together, especially during George's presidency, was a welcome relief from the pressures of the job.

Along the way, Ken has become a part of our family, and both he and his wonderful wife Anne have made life before, during, and after the White House a joy for George and me. So even if I cannot confirm the accuracy of the fish tales that adorn these pages, I can attest that Ken Raynor is, in George's words, "a good man and a treasured friend."

PREFACE:
Meet George Bush
by Michael Patrick Shiels

Michael Patrick Shiels collaborated with Ken Raynor to author I Call Him "Mr. President" *and was an advance volunteer for George H. W. Bush's two presidential campaigns.*

T he lifestyle of "former US president" seems like the best gig in the world, based on what I've seen during my visits to Kennebunkport and in writing the tales Ken Raynor shared for this book.

George H. W. Bush deserves a rewarding post-presidency more than anyone. If you look at his long career in public service, he always seemed willing to take the tougher road. He enlisted in the Navy before the bombs stopped dropping on Pearl Harbor and was shot down in the Second World War.

After earning a degree at Yale, he moved his family from the elite Northeast to the decidedly unglamorous Midland, Texas, to prospect in the oil business.

Give up a safe congressional seat to try to defeat a powerful Senate incumbent? Count him in . . . and after an election loss, out. But never down, because President Nixon rewarded his loyalty by appointing him ambassador to the United Nations.

Then Nixon came calling, asking Bush to take what was a comparatively dirty job: running the Republican National Committee. "When the president asks you, your answer should be yes," he loyally insisted. In time, Bush would have no choice, in his RNC role, but to write a letter to that same president, advising Nixon to resign.

Bush was then reportedly offered his pick of cushy ambassadorships by President Ford. Can you say Paris? Rome? The Maldives? I would have! But not George H. W. Bush—he chose Beijing . . . to be envoy to China.

The CIA was the next challenge George H. W. Bush was asked to fix—with the catch that he be removed from consideration to be President Gerald Ford's vice presidential running mate in 1976. Duty called though, and he accepted the CIA role, since it was the president asking.

After giving Ronald Reagan the run for his life in the presidential primary, he may not have been Reagan's first choice to be his vice president, but he nevertheless served as veep with dignity and complete and utter loyalty, even refusing to land on the South Lawn in a helicopter in the hours after Reagan had been shot and was incapacitated in the hospital. He demanded to be driven from Andrews Air Force Base, instead, insisting "Only the president lands on the South Lawn."

As president he asked America to be a "kinder, gentler nation," and then, due to the respect the world had for his loyalty, was able to build a multi-national coalition, including some strange bedfellows, to free Kuwait after the Iraqi invasion.

When Bill Clinton's election win denied President Bush a second term, he left a letter in the Oval Office desk for Clinton to find which read, in part, "I'll be rooting for you."

Even in retirement, though he certainly didn't have to, President Bush continued to "earn it" through random kindnesses, humility, and insisting on giving back to anyone he met, and countless others by association, in a ripple effect of friendship that reached from sea to shining sea.

I have taken various people to Kennebunkport to participate in the George H. W. Bush Celebrity Golf Classic, a fundraiser organized with such professional passion by my friend Lana Wescott and her event planning company. My mother Gladys was as nervous as a cat to meet Mrs. Bush. She lives in Trenton, Michigan, so she brought a gift for the former first lady: a history book about the Naval Air Station at which President Bush learned to fly in neighboring Grosse Ile. The young Bush couple had also lived where she lives, in Trenton, during the war in 1945 before the president was sent to the Pacific.

When I introduced my nervous mother to Mrs. Bush, "Bar" was so sincere and enthusiastic that she put my mother at ease.

"Your pearls are beautiful," my mother told her.

"Oh these? These are fakes, dear," said Mrs. Bush. "I could never have real pearls like these."

As my mother laughed, Mrs. Bush continued, "Come to think of it, there are a lot of fake things on this ninety-one-year-old body. When I get to heaven God won't even recognize me."

By the time my mother got back to Michigan two days later, a two-page, handwritten thank you letter from Mrs. Bush, recounting elements of their conversation, had already arrived for her!

During the golf outing at Cape Arundel the previous year, my high-school-aged son Harrison was playing in a foursome with me, CBS sportscaster Jim Nantz, and George P. Bush, the president's grandson (Governor Jeb's son).

As Harrison waited at the tee to hit his drive, President and Mrs. Bush and golf pro Ken Raynor pulled up to the tee on golf carts to watch for a bit. Now if it were me waiting to hit the shot in front of them, I would have been unable to breathe and been reduced to a trembling mess of nerves. I would have choked just trying to put my tee in the ground. Nantz hyped the moment even more by launching into his "CBS golf commentator" voice: *"Young Harrison Shiels now must hit this pivotal shot in front of the former leader of the free world . . ."*

The unflappable lad blasted the ball over the hollow to the front of the green! As Harrison got high-fives, George P.'s "Gampy," who had been the 41st president, pulled from the pocket of his windbreaker a small box and gave it to Harrison. In the box was a commemorative golf ball—an autographed "Titleist 41"—with the presidential logo on it.

"Harrison," Nantz intoned, "you may play for a lot of trophies in your life, but you'll never get one as special as you have today."

Ken Raynor has countless expressions of kindness he's received from President Bush—from clipped cartoons, to the watch he wears, and even a fishing boat—but he cherishes the many personal notes and photos he's received from President Bush over more than thirty years just as much. Thank goodness he and his wife Anne so diligently saved, stored, and virtually catalogued crates full of these touching expressions of friendship, some just a handwritten line or two on presidential stationary signed, "Hastily but with best wishes, George Bush."

In this book, Raynor reveals beautifully how President Bush automatically tries to make people he encounters feel special, and provides examples of the president's playful wit.

I witnessed this in action the last time I saw President Bush, in June of 2016, at a small afternoon gathering in Kennebunkport. Before the gathering, I'd found a tiny, vintage "Bush for President" campaign button from his 1988 presidential run, so for fun I wore the button on my lapel. President Bush entered the living room on his motorized wheelchair, having just turned ninety-two years old. I greeted him, and without missing a beat, he noticed the little campaign button and exclaimed, "You're the best dressed man here!"

PREFACE:
Friend First

By Ken Raynor

Ken Raynor, the author, has been friends with President George H. W. Bush and his family for nearly forty years. Raynor is the head golf professional at Cape Arundel Golf Club, in Kennebunkport, Maine, and Coral Creek Club in Placida, Florida, each of which enjoys the membership of the 41st president.

It all started with a statement from the man who would become the 41st president of the United States: "You can learn a lot about a person by playing a round of golf with them or standing in a river casting a fly shoulder to shoulder." Little did I know of the friendship and love that would follow, not to mention the amazing adventures and experiences the future held.

Those who know about my forty-year association with the Bush Family have been saying for years: "Write a book," or "please share these experiences," or "love that story". . . so, here it is!

My two wonderful parents brought me up with many opportunities and instilled the importance of personal values, character, and knowing the difference between right and wrong. I would hear these values preached again during many experiences with Mr. Bush — soon to become Vice President Bush and thereafter "Mr. President."

Day one of this nearly forty-year relationship is hard to pinpoint, but I remember that each and every experience was always full of fun, compassion, and memories that will last a lifetime. There were constant reminders of the complications of the world around us — people with a cause maybe crossing the line to be heard, and the need for security—but these were overshadowed by the caring and passion of my friend the president.

The president said many times to me, "It's just as easy to say 'yes' as it is to say 'no.'" I witnessed this hundreds of times through his actions. When people nervously stood behind security after a round of golf, hoping for a picture, autograph, or handshake, the president would initiate the conversation: "Can we do a picture together?" or "How was your game today?" he would ask. It was always about the other guy, never about the man who held the most powerful position in the world.

I always thought of the man whom I called partner on the golf course as my second dad! Our relationship included many shared adventures made special by people we met and came to know as lifelong friends. Fishing (fly fishing to be more precise) to catch the "fish of a thousand casts": the Atlantic salmon in Labrador and Newfoundland; Arctic char on the famed Tree River in Canada's Northern Territory; or right at home in Kennebunkport for striped bass or bluefish and Florida for snook, redfish, and tarpon: These are the times the president was just "one of the boys." As he would say: "You learn a lot about a person standing in a pair of waders or playing eighteen holes."

Golf, and the many relationships and memories that playing in a four-ball produces, brought us together. Our rounds of golf would be always full of laughter and fun with family, PGA Tour champions, Cabinet members, club members, and longtime friends. Most matches ended with "double-or-nothing" on the eighteenth hole and then maybe a chip-off until the match was even. But we all won, thankful for the memories we shared.

Often the sounds of song filled the end of the day's activities as we sat in the living room, on the floor, without shoes, doing a sing-along with family, friends, and various recording artists. Then it was homeward to bed with many fond memories of the day past and the value of this special shared friendship.

Kennebunkport, for "#41," became known as the president's "Anchor to Windward," a phrase denoting time with family, friends, and a place to decompress. It's hard to say what the exact appeal of Kennebunkport is. It may be the sound of the crashing surf outside the bedroom window, or the exhilaration of wearing that cold Maine sea spray while navigating the numerous lobster pots driving the family's speedboat *Fidelity*. Whatever it is, it works for all of us who are called locals, summer residents, or those who on vacation decide that their road travels through town. The Bush Family is passionate about their love of Maine. President Bush has been there every year of his life but one, a tradition that has carried through to today with the rest of the family. George W., Jeb, Neil, Marv, and Doro and their families cherish their time in Maine, along with Mom and Dad. For all of the years that I've been a part of this family affair, it has been a schedule of consistent activities and competitions: a workout in the morning, tennis to follow, then office time, lunch, eighteen holes of golf, and a boat ride, horseshoes, and dinner to end the day. Just thinking about that makes me exhausted!

"Time Shared" could have been the title of this book, because President Bush's and Bar's custom of extending invitations to many different people without ever excluding anyone was an art form. He has always had great love for our locals: Sonny of "Port Lobster"; Booth Chick (owner of the marina); lifelong friends Spike and Betsy Heminway; Barry and Sandy Boardman; and longtime Cape Arundel members/club presidents Ken Raynor (no relation), Bill Matthews, Bill Cox, Gary Koch, and Pierce O'Neil. Whether the activity was golf, tennis, or boat rides, the president was always happy to share it with folks from all walks of life whom he considered true friends.

The real author of this book is Michael Patrick Shiels, a now lifelong friend who is dedicated to the good in life. He has featured many of the personalities in this book on his *Michigan's Big Show* morning radio program, heard on eleven radio stations weekdays from 6:00 to 9:00 a.m. His passion for storytelling is evidenced by his nine previous books, including collaborations with Donald Trump, Arthur Hills, and Ben Wright. After many seasons working with the PGA Tour and winning Network Radio Personality of the Year, Michael Patrick continues to make a contribution in charity work and helping others. This is where our story started, when we joined forces in the George Bush Cape Arundel Celebrity Classic to raise money for Gary's House, which still operates today. From the moment he met President Bush, Michael Patrick could see and sense the special bond shared between a president and a club professional. Thank you, Michael, for making this bond come alive on the page! Thanks also to Tracy Brennan of Trace Literary Agency and to our Skyhorse editor, Julie Ganz.

I hope you enjoy reading about the cherished moments I shared with George H. W. Bush and the Bush Family.

1
DESPERATE DIPLOMACY

Have you ever felt awkward when you were the first one to arrive at a dinner party?

Not at the Bushes' home.

Barbara Bush set us at ease when my wife Anne and I arrived in the living room of the Bushes' oceanfront home on rocky Walker's Point in Kennebunkport, Maine.

We were the first to arrive, and Mrs. Bush appeared truly delighted to see us when we walked into her living room. It's important to know if the Bushes ever invite you to their home at 6:00 p.m., being "fashionably late" is not fashionable at all. To the Bushes, if you're five minutes early you're right on time.

Other past presidents, the 42nd president for instance, developed a reputation for running behind. But not #41. If he made a 10:00 a.m. tee time at Cape Arundel Golf Club, for instance, where I am head professional, he'd usually be there and ready to go twenty minutes before. We always anticipated early arrivals for everything he was involved with, and if we were invited to the Bushes' home at 6:00 p.m., we were sure to pass through the front gate exactly at 6:00 p.m., as we did on this warm July night.

Earlier that day a couple of PGA Tour players and their wives had come into town for a weekend of fun, friendship, and golf at the invitation of President Bush. I welcomed the president with Major Championship winners Phil Mickelson, Justin Leonard, and Davis Love III to Cape Arundel, just a few miles from Walker's Point, in mid-morning. The four of them played eighteen speedy holes of golf.

As our guests soon learned, they don't make them like Cape Arundel anymore. It's an old Walter Travis redesigned (in 1919) par-69 course with a clubhouse housing simple locker rooms and a food service menu consisting of coffee out of a Keurig machine. Cape Arundel is pure golf, as we golfers call it "hallowed ground" — a links-style course with the Kennebunk River running throughout with tiny, terraced green complexes and chocolate-drop mounds that Travis, himself, said "will challenge players at every level." Our guests quickly experienced the same joy of the game that many past historic figures, including Charles Lindbergh and Babe Ruth, have experienced and embraced. The club, still today, is open for guest play and vacationers who might even see a president!

While it is a different experience than they are used to, the world-class players who come here love it. It is heartwarming to see PGA Tour players actually "playing" a game here on one of the oldest courses in Maine (est. 1896). They compete professionally at big-name courses such as Augusta National or Pebble Beach, and yet they understand this is a special place that has an old-time, relaxed aura of its own.

Leonard, Love, and Mickelson completed a quick round with President Bush and headed back to his house on Walker's Point for lunch and the promised fishing.

The Walker's Point compound of the Bush Family homes is on an eleven-acre peninsula jutting out into the sea, and the dock is protected in the cove next to where President Bush's boat *Fidelity* is moored. The various family homes, the dock, and the boat are all visible from Ocean Avenue or by boaters who happen by, including the Rugosa Lobster Boat, which ferries tourists by for photos every few hours.

After waving goodbye to their motorcade, I finished up my day's work at the course and, at day's end, went home to clean up for the dinner party and celebration the president was throwing in honor of Mickelson, Leonard, Love, their wives, and other friends at 6:00 p.m.—the party at which Anne and I were chatting with a suddenly pensive First Lady Barbara Bush.

The president's nephew Hap and his wife Robin Ellis arrived at the dinner party next. It was around this time that Mrs. Bush got another update from one of the house stewards, a message she shared with us without the smile returning to her face: "George is still aboard the boat and out there somewhere . . . but he sent word that he's on his way back," she said. She was among friends, so she didn't need to conceal her displeasure. "Bar" was not happy because the president had twenty guests about to arrive, including the houseguest wives of the Tour players, and the host, her husband, was nowhere to be found. In fact, he was miles out at sea! She was . . . not happy!

The president, at the wheel of *Fidelity*, in the element he loves, took Mickelson, Leonard, and Love thirteen miles offshore out to Boone Island. Apparently they'd "gotten into some fish," which was good and very exciting for them, but less so for Mrs. Bush.

Having been on that boat, and under the circumstances, I can imagine what that ride back from Boone Island must have been like. The president had gotten the word that all of the guests were at the party and that Bar was not happy. Now that the president knew he had to get back in a hurry, he likely drove that boat sixty miles an hour over thirteen miles of Atlantic Ocean with the PGA Tour players and a Secret Service agent onboard. That had to be a ride only a fighter pilot would enjoy! And a ride that in no way could the Secret Service Zodiac chase boat keep up with. The president's boat usually goes faster than the Secret Service boat, and he really loved speed, so sometimes the agents struggled to keep up because their boat was not as comfortable as his. And sometimes he seemed to enjoy, on the way home from a fishing trip, putting the pedal to the metal and trying to beat the agents home. It was that competitive streak in him. He was just trying to have a little fun on the sea.

But this time here was, all rolled into one, a veteran of the Second World War, the nation's youngest-ever naval aviator, a Yale University graduate who played collegiate baseball, successful Texas oilman, former member of the US Congress, US ambassador to the United Nations, chairman of the Republican National Committee, US envoy to China, director of the Central

Intelligence Agency, former US vice president . . . the former commander-in-chief and leader of the free world, hustling home from a fishing trip, like any other man, because he was in trouble with his wife.

I watched Mrs. Bush as the steward returned occasionally to whisper updates to her about the president's progress in returning and how many minutes out he was. The roomful of guests were enjoying themselves, and Bar, always the gracious host, kept up a lively conversation, but I could tell it was with "an eye to the sea" wondering just when George would arrive home. Someone asked a question and I heard Bar reply, "George is on his way home, but it is very rude that he's out somewhere on his boat when he should be welcoming guests."

People smiled at the thought of President Bush having fun.

Eventually word finally arrived that his fishing party had pulled up to the dock. The din of people talking during the polite party was suddenly interrupted by a clamor. The front door swung open. Everyone stopped talking and looked over at the noisy entrance.

President George H. W. Bush came through the door . . . in his rumpled fishing clothes with windblown hair. He looked like he'd come straight out of a Bass Pro Shops catalog. With a gleam in his eye, the president held up a string of freshly caught, smelly mackerel.

"Barbie," he cried out to Mrs. Bush while holding up the fish and trying not to grin, "I brought you a peace offering!"

Uproarious laughter came from everybody except Mrs. Bush, who sent him immediately for a shower and to change (though she may have been trying not to break a smile—remember, when asked about her husband, she was once quoted as answering, "you just have to adore someone who adores you").

Ten minutes later, President Bush made another head-turning entrance. This time "Dapper Dan" returned to the very cordial gathering of friends squeaky clean but nonchalantly wearing an audacious, purple, sequined coat with the inside lined by a patriotic American flag print silk. I believe the jacket had been given to him by the Oak Ridge Boys.

With jaws dropped and smiles all around, the real "party at the Point" had begun! Welcome, Mr. President, to your party!

2

SO YOU WANT TO PLAY GOLF WITH A PRESIDENT?

I'm a bit embarrassed to admit it, but I really, honestly don't remember the first time I met George Bush.

I completed my bachelor's degree at Nasson College, in Springvale, Maine, and opted to stay in Maine over the summer months during those years. Cape Arundel Golf Club initially hired me to work on the course as a member of the maintenance crew. In subsequent summers, I moved into the club's golf shop to work for head professional Bryce Roberts. After graduating from college, I decided to make golf my career. Roberts hired me as his assistant and, when he left Cape Arundel for another job in 1979, I was promoted to head professional.

George Bush was a "celebrity" member of the club. But interestingly, and I think it's fair to say, that he was notable because of his own accomplishments (wartime, business, political, diplomatic, etc.), even though he was coming to the club as part of the dynasty of the Walker/Bush Family. The core of the club for many years prior to World War II, the Bush/Walker family was vested in Cape Arundel. His father, Prescott Bush, was USGA president and a US senator. His maternal grandfather, George Herbert Walker, also a USGA president, was the donor of the Walker Cup—the amateur version of the Ryder Cup—in which American players compete against the best players from Great Britain and Ireland.

What I do recall about initially meeting Mr. Bush is that it was around the time that he had begun seeking the Republican nomination for president, and that he was friendly, likable, and very engaging. He made me feel like I knew him his whole life and that he was a friend after a very short time together. He always made me feel he had time for me (not that I ever tried to take any of his time). He was clearly a member of the "Greatest Generation." People have always been important to him, which is why he's dedicated his career to serving other people. Those of us at Cape Arundel are lucky enough to have been embraced by him.

When Mr. Bush ran for the nomination in 1980, we had a vested interest because our friend was running for the presidency and it was happening "right on our front porch." Since the Second World War, golfers have beaten non-golfers in sixteen of eighteen presidential elections, with Jimmy Carter and Harry Truman being the exceptions.

I was completing my first year as head golf professional in 1979. Little did I know that one day I'd be dubbed "the President's Pro," or, as Geoff Hobson wrote in the *Portland Press Herald*, "Secretary of Swing." I certainly couldn't have fathomed the fact that, during a makeshift press gaggle on the first tee at Cape Arundel, a reporter, wondering whom President Bush would nominate for an opening on the Supreme Court, shouted, "Is it Ken Raynor? Are you vetting Raynor?"

A phone call like that never came, but getting a phone call from the president of the United States, no matter how many times I got one, and no matter what it was about, was always a touch surreal. On one hand, I was excited to be hearing from my friend. On the other hand, the manner in which it happens is a reminder that your friend is the commander-in-chief and, as such, is the leader of the free world.

There was no caller ID when the phone rang in the late 1980s, and so it was always a surprise when I'd pick up the handset, put it to my ear, say "hello," and hear an official, distant voice ask, "Is this Mr. Ken Raynor?"

"Yes it is."

"Please hold. The president of the United States is calling."

If the president was away from the White House, his personal aide would place the call.

The next voice I heard would be the president himself.

"Kenny? George Bush here!"

Mrs. Bush referred to herself by her first name, too. She always made a point of insisting to friends, "My name is 'Bar.'" If someone close to her calls her "Mrs. Bush," she doesn't like it. By the same token, if someone she doesn't know gets too familiar or casual and calls her Barbara, she might just shoot them one of her famous, pointed glances. Furthermore, at cocktail parties and mixers, when someone standing for a photo with Mrs. Bush is wearing a name tag, I have seen her pluck it off their lapel.

"You don't need this. I think you know who you are," Mrs. Bush jokes.

Early in our relationship, Vice President Bush, in a foreshadowing of the adventures he'd include me in, called me and had me meet him in Washington, DC to play golf at Burning Tree Country Club with Jay Sigel, the great amateur player who later in life competed on the Senior PGA Tour. Sigel, from Pennsylvania, had won back-to-back US Amateur Championship titles in 1982 and 1983 and had played on nine Walker Cup teams.

After the round, I wasn't sure what would happen next.

"I've got to go back to work at the White House, Kenny," he explained. Then he said, "C'mon, let's go!"

It was suddenly Take Your Golf Professional to Work Day, I guess, as we climbed into the limousine and were driven over to the White House. The vice president walked me into the historic building, which was buzzing in midday like a beehive. He was personally showing me the Cabinet Room and many of the different offices, including the one across the hall used by the inner circle.

A hurried aide then approached Vice President Bush.

"Mr. Vice President, you're scheduled for a meeting in the Oval Office and it's time to go. The president is already in the room, sir."

The vice president nodded and turned to me.

"Ken, I've got to go! Just go down the hall and take a left. Somebody will find you."

With that, he was gone.

It was a funny feeling being in the Oval Office area of the White House — where the actual inner workings of the presidency took place — all by myself.

It was only then I realized I had no credentials. I was just a guy now walking aimlessly around inside the White House, with no introduction and no I.D. I was holding my breath just waiting for someone to approach me.

"Who are you?" "What are you doing here?" "How did you get in here?" I imagined they'd ask me as they nabbed me.

Fat chance they'd believe me when I answered, "Oh, I am a friend of the vice president. I just walked in here with him."

Luckily the officials, likely with the use of cameras, already knew exactly who I was and where I was. An aide came up to me and politely introduced himself and "offered" to escort me to the car and ultimately back to the Naval Observatory, the home of the vice president.

"Had you been four steps quicker around the corner you would have come face to face with President Ronald Reagan," the aide told me as we walked through the labyrinth of corridors and stairways. I never did meet President Reagan. It would have been a big honor.

When the aide and I emerged in the afternoon sunlight, I was put into a black car and driven to the official residence of the vice president—One Observatory Circle—at the Naval Observatory in northwest Washington, DC, where I was to spend the night as Vice President and Mrs. Bush's guest.

The residence on the property was a nice place to wait while Vice President Bush had his meeting with President Reagan and other officials. It's a lovely, old, nineteenth-century Victorian home built in 1893 with beautiful grounds surrounding it. There's plenty of room for outside activities and even a track you can walk on.

"Veeps" started living in the home in 1977, when President Jimmy Carter's vice president, Walter Mondale, moved in. It had become too expensive for the Secret Service to provide protection at private residences, which is where vice presidents who preceded Mondale lived.

When his workday was done, Vice President Bush picked me up and we went out to dinner at Morton's Steakhouse. It was kind of fun to be out to dinner in public with the vice president of the United States.

The next morning I took a walk with Mrs. Bush around the grounds of the Naval Observatory. The vice president's agenda had him flying somewhere that day, so I remember the choppers coming in to pick him up on the Observatory lawn. It was a big deal to see the choppers coming and going. There was a lot of preparation and security and a fire truck and emergency vehicles in case anything went wrong or there was an incident. It was enlightening to see the process, a reminder that my friend was a very important man.

Little did I know the day would come, in the not too distant future, that Vice President Bush would be President Bush, and not only would he take me back into the White House, but also that he'd take me with him aboard one of those choppers, too, right from his own house in Kennebunkport.

At the time, former congressman Jock McKernan was the governor of Maine. During his first term as governor, he married US senator Olympia Snowe, also of Maine. Jock is an avid golfer and I still see him regularly. Through his association with the president, McKernan, who served two terms, has become a friend.

When McKernan, a Republican, was running for reelection in 1990, a fundraiser was held for him at The Woodlands golf course in Falmouth, near Portland. President Bush, who was in office at the time and vacationing in Kennebunkport, agreed to attend. The president asked me if I'd like to come with him. Of course I agreed. The aura of his presidency and everything that came with it was still very new to me, so I knew it would be an interesting and fun experience, and I was happy to maybe find a way to help out while I was there.

I went down to Walker's Point, as instructed, and we took off from the helicopter pad next to the president's home on *Marine One*, the president's helicopter. It was a short flight, but what a "wow" experience it was! Just flying on any aircraft over the ocean is a beautiful experience, but to do it aboard *Marine One* with the president of the United States? It's the kind of thing you see on television—but I just happened to be part of the script at that time. And I was just a humble golf pro!

The pilot was in his dress uniform and, once we entered the aircraft, the president climbed into a big leather chair with the Seal of the President of the United States on it. There is usually more than one chopper that goes, to transport the media and Secret Service, so it creates quite a scene.

We flew the thirty-five miles to The Woodlands and landed to a lot of pomp and circumstance. We were greeted by the governor and the course's golf professional, and many other people. It was fulfilling to see how excited the people were to catch a glimpse of the president and have a moment to remember for a lifetime. As a PGA golf professional, it made me proud to see golf celebrated in this manner, among such important people.

During the golf round, the president and governor went around on a golf cart and greeted each group of players, hitting a shot with them and leaving behind a souvenir or two. My responsibility was to meet, greet, and share a Bush experience and hit a golf shot for each group that came though. If they liked my tee shot, and didn't hit a better one, they could use it as their own. Believe it or not, I still have the logoed golf shirt they gave me on that special day!

About midway through his presidency, President Bush brought a special guest—a colleague, of sorts—to Maine. Cape Arundel Golf Club hosted both the sitting president (I prefer the term "serving president") and the vice president when Dan Quayle, formerly a US senator from Indiana, came to visit Kennebunkport in July of 1990.

When the president and vice president teed it up together that day, they asked me and National Security Advisor Brent Scowcroft to fill out the foursome.

"Kenny what is that contraption behind the clubhouse?" President Bush asked before we went to the first tee.

"It's called the 'Swing Trainer,' Mr. President. Let's take a few minutes and I will show you how it works."

He loved gadgets and contraptions, and at the time the "Swing Trainer" was the granddaddy of them all in golf. It's a seven-foot-tall vertical circle of pipe, on an angle, designed to help golfers with their swing-plane. Golfers stand within it and swing a club along the circle over and over again to create the feel of a proper swing. They can visually see it and kinesthetically feel the proper swing. The plane of the swing can be adjusted according to the height, posture, and flexibility of the person.

President Bush played along and climbed into the circle to give it a try while Vice President Quayle and General Scowcroft looked on.

During the round I saw that Vice President Quayle was an excellent ball-striker. He was two- or three-under-par when we reached the ninth hole. At Cape Arundel when the president played, the press was allowed to ask questions and watch at the first tee and near the ninth green. When the four-ball approached the ninth green in view of the media, Vice President Quayle, very uncharacteristically, chunked a couple of poor shots. He had otherwise played flawlessly through the front nine leading up to that point. I wondered if perhaps even just the presence of the media had gotten into his head. After all, since the day he had been selected as the running mate, the young, conservative Quayle had been exposed by the press for some gaffes, including the "potatoe" misspelling mistake (which was not his fault).

I really enjoyed our time on the golf course. Vice President Quayle was very cordial, and I certainly see why President Bush gave him continued support. Watching them together was rewarding, as they were able to relax and enjoy themselves. While the round was competitive, let's face it, the vice president was playing with "the boss" and his host, and it was his club, so I got the sense he was very appreciative to be there and in turn particularly respectful.

Dan Quayle, Former Vice President of the United States

While we were in office, the president and I didn't think it was a good idea, because of the optics, to be seen playing golf together, but there was one exception when I played golf with him at Cape Arundel Golf Club in Kennebunkport. There are no practice swings. No mulligans on the first tee, either.

We finished and I said, "Well, that was a quick round!"

The president asked, "How long did it take?"

I answered, "Two hours and forty-five minutes."

He said, "Well, that's pretty good."

Then I asked the president what everybody shot.

The president answered, "We don't care what anybody shoots; it's just about how long it takes to play."

For him, as long as it takes under three hours, it's like breaking 80!

Once, after we'd completed our time in office, President Bush phoned and said that he'd been invited to play in the AT&T Pebble Beach National Pro-Am.

"Should we go?" he asked me.

I told him, "It's a wonderful tournament. You're going to see a lot of your friends. I think that we should go, but I am warning you, it's a six-hour round of golf."

"For thirty-six holes?" he asked. "I thought it was only eighteen each day?"

"Six hours for eighteen holes," I explained.

We went and played in the Pebble Beach tournament anyway.

I played in the group behind former president Bush at Spyglass Country Club, which is one of the courses they use during the event. On the first hole I hit my second shot off to the right. I went under the rope into the gallery to find my ball and someone said, "Hey, your boss was just here!"

"Oh you mean here in the rough," I asked.

"Yeah," the spectator answered.

"How's he doing?" I wondered.

"Well he's having a lot of fun, but he just hit someone."

"Whoops, that's not good!" I said.

He must have hit someone with a shot on the very first hole, a la Gerald Ford!

But not all of my fond memories of George H. W. Bush come from our experiences on the golf course, or even while discussing official business.

One particular memory strikes me. We were still in office right after my wife Marilyn had surgery. President Bush said to me, "Look, why don't you take her and your family and go up to Camp David? Barbara and I were thinking about going up this weekend, but why don't you just take it and go up there?"

I said, "There's enough room for you as well."

He said, "No, no you guys need it. Why don't you just take it?"

That's the kind of person he is. Very sweet.

I was the luckiest vice president in the history of the office. Former president George H. W. Bush is an honest, decent, caring, hard-working, intelligent person who was a great leader. He'd been vice president for eight years, so he knew the office. He was a wonderful person. I have told my children if you want a role model in life, President Bush is your person.

The "Veep" and the "Prez," Dan Quayle and George Bush, on the first tee. Love the president's cap emblazoned with the name of my fishing boat Fin-addict. (White House Photo)

But my memories on the golf course extend beyond my playing days with H. W. In fact, I've had many opportunities to play golf with Governor Jeb Bush, Marvin, Neil, Doro, and many more times now with the 43rd president, George W. Bush. And like my friendship with his father, my relationship with George W. Bush also grew far beyond the golf course.

In fact, I got to know "W." best before his political career took off. Baseball brought us together. He was part owner of Major League Baseball's Texas Rangers and their spring training home was in Port Charlotte, Florida, very near where I worked winters in Boca Grande.

When my son Kyle was about eight years old, I'd take him over to see the Rangers play a Grapefruit League game and often we'd end up sitting with W., who knew us from Cape Arundel Golf Club in Kennebunkport and was aware of my relationship with his father. We had some nice interaction there.

Shortly after that, W. became governor of Texas.

In later years still, I had the opportunity to share the overall presidential experience with my family when I was able to schedule a private tour of the White House and actually go into the Oval Office to meet the 43rd president, George W. Bush. I took my sister Janice Giegler, who was in the Connecticut State House of Representatives, and her husband Tom; my dad, Russ, who served as a Marine in the Philippines repairing hydraulic systems on airplanes during the Second World War; and my mom, Harriet, who was an executive secretary when she was not being a mother. They got a chance to feel what I felt over the years: a close, personal association with a president of the United States.

We made it just under the wire, as it was "#43"'s eighth year in office, and President Obama had just been elected. After we walked into the Oval Office, and the introductions were made, my father spoke up.

"What are we in for with the new president?" my dad asked President Bush.

President Bush looked at my father, with a half-grin and his trademark squint, and said, "Well, Mr. Raynor, I have learned three things as president of the United States: You have to have a lot of faith; you have to have good people around you and be a good listener; and you have to be a decision-maker. If President-Elect Obama has all of those, we'll be just fine."

President George W. Bush now spends all of January in Boca Grande, Florida, after the annual family Christmas reunion there. #43 enjoys playing golf at Coral Creek Club, where I serve as the head golf pro, and also plays at the Gasparilla Inn. He's a student of the game of golf and plays a lot of golf near his home in Texas with Major champions David Graham and Lee Trevino. The president practices more than he ever has, and it shows.

President George H. W. Bush opened the door for me to some unique experiences, and I tried, in turn, to include others who I knew would appreciate such experiences as well. For example, my father-in-law, Chuck Forrest, was an avid golfer. Therefore, it was a real joy when the day came for me to introduce Chuck, who had been a golf nut all of his life, to Arnold Palmer, who had been invited by the president to visit. There Chuck stood on the porch at Cape Arundel—where his son-in-law was the head professional—talking with "The King" and the president, too! On other occasions, I invited old friends for a round of golf and surprised them by having the president of the United States join them.

Palmer and the president on the porch with my father-in-law Chuck Forrest and my parents Russ and Harriet Raynor beside my sister Janice Giegler. (*White House photo*)

My friend Ted Marschke is one such example. He and I went to John Jay High School together in Westchester County, New York. Our golf team was a powerhouse, but I was just starting my golf career. I didn't know much about the game and had never really been exposed to it, but for some reason I was attracted to it. Nobody in my family, to this day, plays golf. Nobody, literally, even though I am a descendant of Seth Raynor, the famed Golden Age golf course architect. Raynor, a Princeton alum, died in Palm Beach in 1926, but not before building about a hundred golf courses in a twenty-year career. His most famous creations include Chicago Golf Club; Fishers Island Club in New York; two courses at The Greenbrier in West Virginia; Yale Golf Club; Mountain Lake in Lake Wales, Florida; and Waialae Golf Club in Honolulu.

Ted, though, was a good player. He made the team all four years and was one of the top-ranked players on the team. My friends and I would drag Ted out of bed by playing a game of "fumble" (throwing a football on the bed and then all jumping on the bed to recover the football) and off we would go to a course called James Baird Golf Course, a public course on the Taconic State Parkway, for an afternoon of golf. Ted would typically shoot his 72 and I'd shoot my 92.

Eventually we both went off to college, and because I worked on my game and played more golf my game greatly improved. By 1976 I'd improved all aspects of my game, so I entered the PGA program to become a certified golf professional. I became the head professional at Cape Arundel in 1979 — where I would spend the next thirty-eight or more years becoming the longest-serving golf professional in the club's history.

It was right about this time that I'd reconnected with good old Ted "Fumble" Marschke. He and his wife decided to come up for a visit and Ted was hoping, like the old days, we might play some golf. I told Ted to meet me at Cape Arundel at 1:00 p.m. on a Friday.

I knew, because the White House had alerted me in advance, that President Bush was coming into town for the weekend, and thus I figured he'd want to play golf, too.

"Mr. President, if you don't have another person to play with us, I will have a dear friend from high school coming to visit. Would you mind if he joined us?" I asked.

"Bring him on, Kenny. Let's see if he's got any game," he answered. He was, as usual, excited about sharing.

I said nothing to Ted about who we would be playing golf with on Friday.

When the day came, Ted arrived early for our 1:00 p.m. starting time. He began to notice a lot of security people moving about, and he quickly figured out who we'd be playing with.

On the first tee, I got to introduce the man who introduced me to golf, thereby giving me a career, to the president of the United States for a round of golf I know he will never forget.

Was Ted nervous?

If you call his jowls shaking "nervous," then yes!

I tried to calm him down a little, as I do with others who join the president for golf, by just telling him what to expect and how the process would go. Mainly it was to explain that President Bush plays very quickly and it's best to keep up the pace. (I also told them this for President Bush's sake. I didn't want him to be waiting around on a pokey player.)

The president is very good on the golf course. He is very comforting to people he plays with because he understands the situation they're put in. He understands that playing golf with the president isn't the most relaxing thing you can do. As much as Ted was excited and grateful, he was nervous as a cat.

President Bush, always by unanimous insistence of the foursome, hits the first tee shot, as he did this day. But first he paused to make an announcement.

"I am hereby instilling 'Rule 35-4!'" he pronounced, holding a finger in the air as if it were a solemn presidential privilege or Executive Order.

I wondered what he was talking about since, as a PGA professional, I knew golf has only 34 rules.

"Rule 35-4 is the No Laughing Rule," he continued.

Of course then everyone laughed.

The self-deprecating humor broke the ice a little and lowered expectations for President Bush's own pending drive, which I suspect he didn't mind either. Put yourself in his shoes: Every time he went out for a casual game of golf, the eyes and lenses of the media, Secret Service agents, aides, playing partners, his golf professional, and anyone who gathered around the first tee were upon him. The last thing they want to see the leader of the free world do is top a shot into the weeds or God forbid "whiff."

But then, in the middle of all that, after delivering his golf rule joke, President Bush did what I have seen him do countless times. In what seemed like one flowing motion, President Bush, a collegiate baseball player, fighter pilot, and determined leader, took his stance over the ball, gripped his club, set his jaw, focused his steely eyes, and swiped a drive that sailed against the blue afternoon sky straight down the middle and bounded up the fairway.

"Take a bite out of that one!" the president shouted. "Mr. Smooth is back!"

People clapped and laughed.

Ted, on the other hand, given all his nerves, didn't hit a very good first drive. The competitive part of me, after losing to Ted so many times all those years, wanted to give him "some mileage" (if you know what I mean) on the tee about his poor shot. I wanted to tease him. But the other part of me, as a golfer and a grateful friend, wanted him to play well. Ultimately, we gave him a mulligan, which he striped down the middle, and he played very well the rest of the afternoon.

There are usually people around who want autographs or photos during his golf rounds, and President Bush understands that.

Often, because of how quickly the president played, and for security reasons, our foursome would "play through" others on the course. While I am certain the Secret Service would rather have closed the course to outside and even member play when President Bush was out there, he insisted that he not disrupt play and that Cape Arundel remain open to others.

President Bush enjoyed driving the golf cart, since he hadn't driven his own vehicle, other than his boat, in years. On one occasion at the third hole, as we played through a foursome of players who had been in front of us, he surprised me by steering our cart toward the fellows who had pulled off to the side in the rough under a tree.

"Thanks, fellas. Sorry to get in your way," President Bush called out as we pulled up. The golfers were grinning from ear to ear as he quickly shook each of their hands. They were then startled, but delighted, to hear him ask, "Can you guys do me a favor? Would you mind if I got a photo with your foursome?"

"Sure," said one of the players, "that'd be great!"

They were so excited and began to line up with him to "honor his request" when President Bush had to ask, "Do you mind if we use one of your cameras?" (Believe me, over the years of playing golf with the president as a PGA professional, I learned how to take photos with a lot of different types of cameras and cell phone cameras! I've even been asked, in a pinch, to take a photo with an iPad.) I took the photo—and the guy in the picture with the biggest grin was President Bush. We then zipped away to play on.

About three holes later we came up to another foursome.

"Thanks, men. Sorry to get in your way," he said again, only slowing the cart this time but smiling at and waving to each of the yielding players. He then tossed a small box to a tall man with glasses who was caught off guard. The president instructed him, as we drove off, "Whoever makes the longest putt on this hole gets that!"

Inside the little cardboard cube box was a souvenir golf ball with the presidential seal printed on it and signed "George Bush." He was thoughtful to carry these around with him for such occasions to show his appreciation.

On many occasions where we'd be coming in off the golf course, talking about the match, taking our gloves off, and putting the balls back in the golf bag, there would be a family standing afar with a couple of small kids holding scorecards and pencils. It was like a Norman Rockwell drawing of an all-American family hoping to get an autograph from a star but afraid to approach the person and ask for it. President Bush looked up and called over to them. "Hey, would you mind if I signed your scorecard?"

Again he invited them into his circle, at a time when they were unsure if it was okay to come over or whether the Secret Service would allow them to. His warmth instantly shined through. Imagine what that did, for that moment in time, for that family standing there. It's a moment they will never forget.

As far as President Bush the golfer, I have learned lessons from him that I will take with me the rest of my life.

Take his golf lingo, for instance. If he took a little off the shot I'd hear, "I put a little feather on that one!" Sometimes it would be, "I put a cut on that," as he called his shots.

He was big on making "dedications," too, to his son Marvin or other family members and friends. Before hitting a shot he would say something like, "I hereby dedicate this shot to my wife Barbie!" If it turned out to be a good shot, he'd proudly tout the phrase "take a bite out of that one, Bar!" If the shot were poor, perhaps finishing in a water hazard, he would quickly say, "Sorry, Barbie. I sure hope you can swim!"

After my son Kyle was born, I handed out cigars, with a blue (to signify "it's a boy!") trout fly tied to them. But I also gave away golf balls with Kyle's name and his birthdate stamped on them. Many rounds later, at Cape Arundel the president reached into his golf bag, pulled out a ball, looked at it, and realized it was the "Kyle ball."

"I dedicate this next shot to the "Big Guy" Kyle Raynor!" the president pronounced.

The ball brought him luck because he played very well with it during that round. But when we got to the thirteenth tee, which is a 165-yard, par-3 hole with water on the left side and in front of the green, the president looked at the hole and paused before hitting his tee shot.

"I don't want to lose the 'Kyle ball,'" he said. Then he looked at me and said, "But Kyle is a survivor!"

He swung the club and knocked the Kyle ball up into the green.

We played golf often with a great friend of the president's named Spike Heminway, who would join the president in delighting in playful golf clichés:

"The Vomit Zone" was the way to describe a putt which was just short — but long enough to make a grown man nervous.

"The Volume Button" was a way to tell a player they were doing more "big talking" than they were producing big shots. Or it was meant to jab back at a player who was chattering, in an attempt to get into their head to distract them and make them miss a putt.

"Vic Damone!" is what the president might shout out for a "victory" small or large! This exclamation was also used during spirited horseshoe competitions.

Sometimes on the golf course we'd play for a dollar or a dime, but what President Bush is really known for is that it's always "double or nothing" on the eighteenth hole—no matter what! If you still owe a dime after the eighteenth hole, we'd usually play one more hole or we'd have a chip-off. Most of the time at the end of the round nobody owed anybody anything. Very civilized, right? Remember, presidents are great negotiators.

In other words, he would have fun with the game of golf right from the start, which was endearing to anyone playing with him who might be nervous. After all, you never know how anxiety can impact your game—especially when you're dealing with a powerful world leader. But President Bush has shown over and over he loves to have fun with people.

One of the first times he came to play golf at Cape Arundel as president serves as a great example of his nature. On this particular occasion, we had reached the third hole, which is a great par-3 with a false front to the green. The left side of the hole is very elevated with about a twenty-foot drop next to a tidal brook that runs through there. It's the site of an old grist mill.

The water really shouldn't come into play, but the president hit his tee shot and the ball hit the edge of the rocks and seemed to trickle down by the water. He went to look for his ball, and I went to help him try to find it.

He spotted a ball on the riverbed about two feet out beyond the tidal mark and there were a couple of little rocks out there he could step on to reach it, so he wanted to go out there and pick up his ball. The Secret Service agents were concerned.

"No, sir, you don't really want to do that, do you? Those rocks look pretty slippery," one of the agents implored.

Upon hearing the agents and nodding, President Bush turned to me with a question.

"Are these shoes waterproof?" After all, a good golf pro always knows which shoe brands are waterproof.

I told him they were.

The next thing I knew the president had stepped out onto the two tiny, six-inch rocks and was trying to stay balanced on them to get his ball. Then I see he's spotted another golf ball while he was out there. Suddenly, President

Bush appeared to have given up on the rocks and started walking in the ankle-deep water in his golf shoes picking up golf balls! He was walking down in the stream while the Secret Service agents trailed him on the bank. His feet were soaking wet, but he was thrilled by the hunt of his salvage operation.

He finally came out of the brook with his treasure of about eight golf balls, proud as a peacock.

"Why would people leave these golf balls here?" he asked.

President Bush had fun with the media, too. He was engaging with the press—especially off-camera. I was amazed at how he knew the beat reporters' names and a little bit about their families. He knew if their families and kids were staying in Kennebunkport with them. They traveled together a lot, so he'd ask about them. He clearly took a vested interest in them.

On another occasion, when the round was over, a big crowd of reporters, with their notepads, cameras, lights, and boom microphones were waiting for us to come over from the eighteenth green to their staging area. President Bush and I got on the golf cart and, with him behind the wheel, he waved to the press.

"Wave to them, too, Kenny," he instructed.

Some of the reporters waved back and, in anticipation, had their pens or microphones in hand, ready to ask their questions. The cameramen had hoisted their lenses in anticipation of our golf cart and the waving president coming their way. Instead, as the president kept waving and smiling, he put the golf cart in reverse so when he stepped on the accelerator pedal, the golf cart went backwards, away from the media people. He continued to smile and wave the farther we got from the media. While they lowered their lenses and expectations, they laughed, too, at his playfulness.

The president found golf to be a relaxing part of his vice presidential and his presidential years. He loves Cape Arundel and has always stated it's his favorite golf course to play, not because it is the best golf course but because it reminds him of family and friends and all the special times he has had there.

For fun, President Bush sometimes would "drop" into the conversation that he was club champion at Cape Arundel Golf Club back when he was twenty-three years old.

"Let's see what the club champion in 1947 can do," he'd joke when standing over a shot or a putt.

"Hey, did you happen to know I was club champion in 1947?" he'd kid someone in a put-on, proud voice of a braggadocio. It was all tongue in cheek, of course.

The funny thing was, he was never able to produce a trophy, so friends teased him that his claim was impossible.

For fun, his friend Phil Morris, who owned an award business, had a trophy made up, dated 1947, and citing the Cape Arundel club champion as George Bush.

President Bush gave the "trophy" to me to display at the club along with a handwritten note that read:

7-27-03
Dear Ken,
Finally, after years of fruitlessly searching, we found the trophy. It was off in the corner of an attic on "The Point." Now, maybe, people will believe me.
G.B. beat Chad Brown 8-up with 7 to play. An eagle putt on 11 did in Chad.

The truth is young George Bush beat the local postmaster by the name of Chad Brown 8-7. The legend created by family to tease the president was that the only reason Bush beat old Chad Brown was that Brown's flask was empty by the eleventh hole!

When President Bush played golf in his later years, he wanted to play well, but that was probably the least of his priorities on the golf course. The reason that he plays so quickly is because he does not understand what taking four practice swings accomplishes when you've got other things to do in your day. He prefers to get up, hit the ball, and go . . . get up, hit the ball, and go. He just hits the putt and enjoys the result. If it's a good putt, his hands go in the air and he celebrates. If it's a bad shot, we all know it, and we move on.

Maureen Dowd, famous columnist for the *New York Times*, in an August 1989 column headlined BUSH IS YIPPING AND CHIPPING IN WEDGE CITY," wrote: "Mr. Raynor says the President often asks for help, saying, 'What do I do here, Kenny?' But then he plays the shot as the pro hurries to give the advice. No Time to Concentrate."

Arnold Palmer, when he came to Kennebunkport, said the fact that President Bush was known for playing very quickly was good for the game of golf because it served as a high-profile example to other golfers that they can keep the game moving. A foursome keeping pace should be able to finish eighteen holes in four hours or less. The president was very helpful in setting an example of that, and the 43rd president, George W. Bush, likes to play that way, too.

Over the multiple rounds #41 and I played, the press started to notice the speediness and referred, in articles, to his game as "cart polo" and "aerobic golf." I had, by then, learned how to accommodate the president's "need for speed." The trick was to hurry to the ball so I could get there with plenty of time to make a good shot . . . and then go like hell from there. We used to say "it takes just as long to hit two bad shots as it does to take your time and hit one good one."

Pete Bevacqua, CEO, PGA of America

It was a great honor having had the opportunity to meet President Bush on a few occasions in the past. A truly memorable day for me occurred in the summer of 2016 at Cape Arundel Golf Club, which happens to be one of my favorite places on earth. I had the distinct pleasure of driving Mrs. Bush in a golf cart for most of the afternoon hours as we toured the course and visited countless groups playing in a charity event to support Gary's House, a charity the Bushes have vigorously supported for years. In addition, during that time I was able to spend quite a bit of time with the president discussing a wide variety of topics that, of course, included the golf! Seeing the relationship that President and Mrs. Bush share, their endless love for one another and their love of the game, was inspiring.

President Bush and his wife, Barbara, are true American heroes and passionate about the game of golf.

On one particular very early morning, just President Bush and I began playing what ended up being a very quick round of golf at Cape Arundel. There was still dew on the ground and the sun was barely up.

Despite the early hour, we were two friends out there in motion. There was a mutual rhythm to it. I went to my ball; he went to his ball. When I was bringing the cart around after putting out, he was on the next tee likely having already hit his drive. One just accelerated the other, and on we moved.

When we left the eighteenth green, one of the Secret Service agents seemed to have some information to give the president. Looking at his watch he said, "Pardon me, sir, but you just played eighteen holes in one hour and twenty-four minutes."

We hadn't set out to break any records. He just enjoys the game that way.

After some of the reporters wrote about our speedy round, I got a call from a columnist.

"I heard about the round you played with President Bush in less than an hour and a half," he told me. "I'd like to come and write a story about it. Can I come to the Cape Arundel course there and try to replicate the record playing on my own?"

He wanted to experience the speed and how it might have been accomplished.

I thought his angle sounded creative and that his experiential column might bring some nice publicity for the game of golf and Cape Arundel, so I invited him to come and try. We agreed on a time and day when the course would be quiet. I checked with our superintendent Brendan Parkhurst because he'd need to know that someone would be flying around out there early in the morning while he's trying to set up the golf course and mow the greens.

When the day came, we sent the reporter off as a single player just after sunrise before anyone else got out on the course. In his speed quest he reached the seventeenth green with forty-five seconds left in order to break the record of eighteen holes in 1:24. At the eighteenth tee, with thirty seconds left to play the final hole, he topped one or two balls into the Kennebunk River in front of the tee trying to play quickly. It was there that his bid, as a single trying to match the record set by two men, came to an end.

In October, customarily, I lead a group of the club's members on a golf trip to Scotland to play in the "International Four Ball," which is played at Gleneagles, Carnoustie, and the Old Course at St. Andrews — three of Scotland's most esteemed golf courses.

Five days before our group was to leave for Scotland, President Bush was traveling to Europe to make some diplomatic appearances in Poland and a few other countries. The president was due to make a stop in St. Andrews to attend the members meeting of the Royal and Ancient Golf Club of Scotland as a way to show his appreciation for being one of only thirteen people in history to be given an honorary membership.

The night before I was to leave for Scotland, I was at home packing. Just as I was trying to close the lid and latches of my suitcase, the telephone rang. I answered to find it was the president calling.

"Kenny, I'm calling from Poland," he said. "You and I are still meeting in St. Andrews in the next day or two, right?"

"Yes, sir. I'm packing now. I leave tomorrow."

"Great," he said. "Would you do me a favor?"

"Sure, anything."

"Would you go down to Walker's Point and get my trench coat? It's hanging in the hall closet. Could you make certain the fur zip-in liner is in the trench coat and can you bring it over to Scotland for me? It's much colder than I expected and I have additional travels."

I chuckled silently but assured him I would bring it.

Now a full, knee-length trench coat doesn't fold up to be very small and weighs about ten pounds with the liner in it. Now I had to figure out how I was going to add this trench coat into the suitcase I had already just been jumping up and down on to try to get closed. Did I need a different suitcase? Was there some of my clothing I could remove in order to happily take the president's trench coat to him?

I figured it out somehow and delivered the trench coat to the president in the "Auld Grey Toon." He was staying in an apartment overlooking the Old Course's eighteenth hole between the green and Rusack's Hotel. He's returned the favor countless times in many ways.

Each year, when I take members to Scotland, President Bush, as an honorary member of the Royal and Ancient Golf Club, is very kind to give me a letter of introduction for the R&A asking the club to extend any courtesies possible. Thanks to this letter, I am always able to extend his graciousness to the fellow golfers and traditionalists, many of whom have never even been to Scotland before, by taking them into the historic R&A Clubhouse and showing them the Trophy Room. It's an extremely special, rare experience.

On one occasion my group and I walked into the R&A Clubhouse and, as I was introducing the group, the secretary was coming down the steps and overheard the conversation.

"Which one of you is Mr. Raynor?" he sternly asked.

"I am. I am Mr. Raynor," I answered politely.

"So you are Mr. Raynor then. Well, Mr. Raynor, you arrive here at the R&A with impeccable credentials. Impeccable credentials!"

The praise came, of course, thanks to the introductory letter from the former president of the United States.

My members still kid me about that one, but they were extra lucky in that moment, because we were even taken upstairs and allowed to visit the Secretaries Balcony outside overlooking the Old Course's first and eighteenth holes. Naturally we followed up with a drink down the street on the corner at the Dunvegan Pub. After all, how can you go to St. Andrews without stopping at the Dunvegan for a pint or a jigger?

I was blessed with another rare golf experience "on our side of the pond" during President Bush's post-presidential years. It all began when Craig Dobbin, a Canadian who was chairman and CEO of CHC Helicopter Company, started inviting us on fishing trips to Labrador. The president would see Dobbin at other times during the year, too, and one day in 2003 they got to talking about golf. Dobbin had taken up golf later in life and he was really getting into it. He mentioned to the president that playing golf at Augusta National was on his "bucket list."

"I'm pretty sure I can make that happen," President Bush assured Dobbin.

I am the most blessed golf professional in America, because I happened to be there at the same time the conversation took place.

"Ken," President Bush asked, "have you ever played Augusta National?"

I told him I hadn't.

"Well, you'll have to go with us," President Bush said.

Not long after that, I got a phone call from the president's office informing me that a date had been set for early December to go to Augusta National to tee it up.

Augusta National, designed by the great amateur Bobby Jones with Dr. Alister MacKenzie in 1933 on the grounds of a nursery two hours east of Atlanta, is probably the most famous and exclusive private golf club in the world. It's been hosting The Masters Tournament since 1934 and even the television viewers can see that not a single blade of grass is out of place throughout the finely manicured, wooded, rolling grounds. So much tradition was running through my mind: the chance to drive up Magnolia Lane and walk across the Hogan and Sarazen bridges over Rae's Creek; and the opportunity to play shots from the same spots generations of great golfers had, such as Sam Snead, Arnold Palmer, Jack Nicklaus, Gary Player, Tom Watson, Ben Crenshaw, and Tiger Woods.

The club is only open about seven months of the year. It closes shortly after The Masters Tournament, which is in early April. The winner receives a green jacket identical to the blazers the members wear when they're on the property. Most of Augusta National's three hundred or so members, who are very successful businessmen and women, don't live anywhere near the club, and only visit periodically or for club events.

President Dwight D. Eisenhower was a member and had various features named for him, including "Ike's Pond," "Ike's Tree," which was a loblolly pine on the seventeenth hole Eisenhower despised and wanted removed (it was felled by an ice storm in 2014), and the Eisenhower Cabin—one of ten such cabins on the property—which was built for General Eisenhower, to Secret Service specifications, when he was elected president.

President Bush had played Augusta as vice president, but never as president.

It was winter in Maine, so I was down working at the Coral Creek Club, near Boca Grande, Florida, when the day came. It worked out well because Dobbin wintered in Reddington Beach, Florida, near St. Petersburg, north of Boca Grande. President Bush happened to be speaking at a conference near Miami at the Ocean Reef Club, so the plan was that Dobbin would come from St. Petersburg via one of his helicopters, pick me up at Coral Creek, and then we'd go meet President Bush in the Miami area.

My bag was packed and ready to go in my golf shop office when I heard the sound of his chopper arriving.

"How about a quick nine before we go?" he asked.

Why not? Great suggestion!

We played nine holes on Coral Creek's beautiful Tom Fazio design. It's a very natural Florida setting with no homes on the course. We zipped around the course, "George Bush–style," and boarded his chopper.

What a thrilling flight it was right through the state of Florida. I sat in the front with the pilot as we flew over the Everglades and into the Miami area. Craig and I had dinner and checked into a hotel near the airport because we were going to meet President Bush first thing in the morning after he'd been driven up from Ocean Reef and get on a private airplane Craig owned.

Craig's office, though, received a call from President Bush's office with an alteration in plans. President Bush needed to attend a memorial mass in Puerto Rico, honoring the late Governor Luis A. Ferre. The president had been very fond of the governor, who had been a member of the Republican National Committee, and admired his civility.

Craig offered his plane to get President Bush from Florida to Puerto Rico and back, so instead of flying from Southeast Florida to Augusta, we lifted off and flew to Puerto Rico.

Upon landing in Puerto Rico, a motorcade and agents picked up President Bush, and Craig and I spent the morning walking around Old San Juan and doing some Christmas shopping.

We'd played a couple of games of cribbage on the jet when the president arrived, ready to go. Next stop: Augusta.

We made it to the gatehouse on Washington Road and turned up Magnolia Lane just as I'd always dreamed of. It was dusk, so we managed to hurry out and have a little putting contest on the practice green.

We lodged, appropriately, in the Eisenhower Cabin, and eventually went into the antique clubhouse—a former plantation house—for dinner. Though the club was exclusive and private, the atmosphere was warm and inviting and the staff was friendly and congenial. There was no pomp and circumstance at all. People came over and said hello to the president, and it seemed, given the nature of the membership, that some of them had met him before. I remember, for instance, that Peter Ueberroth, who had been Major League Baseball's commissioner and managed the Los Angeles Olympic Games, came across the room to visit.

Altogether, the club was a very welcoming experience. In fact, the first morning I walked into the clubhouse dining room at about 7:30 and was greeted immediately.

"Good morning, Mr. Raynor," one of the dining room stewards welcomed me.

I'd never seen this person before and to this day I have no idea how he knew who I was and yet he welcomed me by name — another part of the Augusta experience.

Once he'd seated me at a table, he asked, "What can I get you for breakfast?"

"May I see a menu?" I responded.

"Oh, sir, we don't have menus here. We will get you anything you want."

I'm not sure what I ordered, but I do remember that it was fabulous food.

We walked eighteen holes after breakfast, plus we played a fun round on the par-3 course. The weather was in the 50s, so it was a little cold on the hands, but we were playing Augusta National, so it really didn't matter to us.

I was fascinated by how different the course feels from what you see on television each year during The Masters Tournament.

I got a chance to experience the complexity of the green on the fifth hole, for instance. I also got to learn just how steep it is from the tee down to the green on the sixth hole and how tough that green is sloped right-to-left. Or when the flagstick is in the top right section of the green how hard it is to get the ball to stop on that terrace and, when it doesn't, how it almost trickles all the way down off the speedy green, leaving you with a long, tough putt.

Until you get there you might not realize how much of a dogleg the thirteenth hole really is when the players hit a draw around the corner. Those pine trees on the right are truly looming, but they're much more inviting than Rey's Creek is on the left.

That evening, the dining room was full of hustle and bustle and green-jacketed Augusta National members. As part of the president's party, we were able to get into and see the Champions Locker Room (for Masters

Tournament winners, only). We were given a tour of the Crow's Nest, the iconic cupola atop the clubhouse where the amateurs who play in The Masters Tournament are allowed to bunk during the event. Touring Augusta National's wine cellar — one of the most extensive wine cellars in the world — was an especially interesting treat, as they had just received a delivery of French Bordeaux. We were amongst the prized cases of Lafite Rothschild and the Chateau Latour, and all of the highly rated (and highly priced) wines. I was living the dream of a golfer and of a wine lover.

The following day we walked another eighteen holes, and bid our caddies, who'd been with us for two days, adieu. Those caddies have toted the bags for all manner of interesting people from around the world. To be able to caddy in a group with a former US president was probably top of the list for them.

The president gave each of the caddies, who wore the Augusta National white jumpsuits, a commemorative presidential golf ball, tie tack, or cuff links as a memento. He always carried those types of items with him to hand out to people he thought might like them. As I saw the excitement the caddies expressed at the small tokens President Bush gave them, I was once again reminded of how committed he was to pleasing people and always planned ahead for it.

From there, it was back onto the airplane, and even there it seemed like he always had others in mind. After drifting off for a ten-minute nap I opened my eyes to see that President Bush had pulled out a box of blank note cards with the presidential seal on the top of each card. He was using his downtime on the flight to handwrite thank you notes and messages to friends and people who'd reached out to him or extended some expression of kindness.

In fact, over the course of his life, President Bush had written so many notes that after he left office he published a book featuring a collection of them, titled, *All the Best, George Bush.*

Among my collection of notes from him is one written on stationary with the heading "Aboard Air Force One" across the top with the presidential seal. I'd often receive updates about his golfing trips — the successes and failures. Perhaps my favorite was when he recounted the time, in 1994, that he played golf in Bermuda: "I stunk, per usual, but we had a great time. . . ." Another read, "I turned down playing in the Hope Tournament for mid-

January in spite of passionate appeals from Bob [Hope] himself. Just don't need that 6½-hour game of show biz golf."

His thoughtful nature extended beyond handwritten letters, too. I remember receiving a calendar about New Zealand fishing in the mail once from the president. He must have remembered that I had, in my lifetime, gone to New Zealand fishing, so he thought I might like to see it. Where he got the calendar and why he had it, I had no idea. There was a sticky note on the front of the calendar on which he'd written, "Thought you'd enjoy . . . GB." That's all that was needed, but to this day, I still wonder—how did he have time to think of me and to mail that to me?

Peter Jacobsen, PGA Tour Player and NBC TV Golf Analyst

President Bush; Governor Jeb Bush; Woody Simmons, a Florida businessman who was the lobbyist for Verizon; and I were at a Barbara Bush Foundation of Literacy "Celebration of Reading" event in Naples, Florida. I was honored to be invited to play golf with the president and governor at a course called The Club at Medditera before the dinner.

We played the fastest round of golf I have ever played.

Luckily Woody clued me in ahead of time that President Bush plays "ready golf." My definition of "ready golf" is that when you get to the ball and you're ready to play, you play! It was really enjoyable. We flew around the golf course even with the Secret Service around and the homeowners on site who gathered because they knew the president and governor were playing.

One of the complaints about golf is that it takes too long. Not for us. We hit our tee shots, got to the cart, chipped the balls onto the greens, and putted out. It didn't matter who was "away." We didn't stand on ceremony.

I think the world of the Bush Family. I am very happy to be involved in the "Celebration of Reading."

Robert Kinard, PGA Professional at Gasparilla Inn and Club, Boca Grande, Florida

President Bush as a person is the nicest person I ever played golf with. I am not saying that because he was the president of the United States. I'm saying that because he is the nicest person I ever played this crazy game with. You cannot meet anyone who is as down to earth as he.

I must say I have never had a better time in my life. He didn't have to play or be nice to me, but he went out of his way to do it.

There is only one other person I thought this much of and that would be Bayard Sharp, the owner of the Gasparilla Inn and Club.

I don't believe there will ever be another man like George H. W. Bush.

His friendship to me will never be equal in any man.

As a president he was very good — as a person no one will ever rank him high enough.

I wish I could have been around him more.

3

A KINDER, GENTLER FRIEND

George and Barbara Bush spend the winter months away from Kennebunkport at their home in a small subdivision in Houston, Texas. Their affinity for the Lone Star State dates back to 1948 when the young couple, with a two-year-old George W. in tow, moved from Connecticut to the Easter Egg Row development in Midland, West Texas, to venture into the oil business.

Former President Bush invited me to Houston one winter to represent him as "The President's Pro" in a celebrity charitable golf tournament that Major League Baseball pitcher Roger Clemens, a Houstonian, was hosting. Mr. and Mrs. Bush kindly sent someone to the airport—George H. W. Bush Intercontinental Airport, in fact—to pick me up and drive me to their home, where I visited with them and spent a couple of comfortable nights in the guest room.

We met for morning coffee in the kitchen and shared the individual plans we were each about to set out for that day. I was headed to participate in Clemens's golf tournament. Mrs. Bush planned to attend a meeting for the Barbara Bush Literacy Foundation. President Bush would be, during midday, visiting a hospital at the behest of the Make a Wish Foundation. In

June 1989, during his administration, President Bush had granted the five hundredth wish of a Make a Wish child to meet him at the White House. The young girl had even sat at his desk in the Oval Office.

We made plans to reconvene at the end of our day for cocktails and to go to dinner.

Mrs. Bush allowed me to borrow her Dodge Caravan to drive out to the golf course for the fundraiser. I wasn't sure any golf would be played, though, since some unseasonably cold, wintry weather had descended on the Houston area. Texans aren't used to icy conditions, so they struggle on the roads, which sometimes have gravel strewn on them to attempt to reduce slipping, sliding, and fender-benders. To tell you the truth, I white-knuckled the steering wheel during my drive all the way to the golf course. I was terrified at the possibility of smashing up Mrs. Bush's car. The last thing I wanted to do was to be responsible for even a dent in the former first lady's van!

The bitter weather didn't allow for much golf that day — just a few holes and a fun par-3 shootout with Dallas Cowboys running back Emmitt Smith and some other celebrity athletes. It had been very cold and windy, though, so I was happy to get into the van and park it safely back at the Bushes' home and get myself under a hot shower.

After I thawed out, dried off, and got dressed, I found myself on the couch clutching a cocktail in the Bushes' living room with my friends George and Barbara. President Bush listened intently between sips as Bar described her day and the meeting she attended. Then he wanted me to tell him all the details about Roger Clemens's golf tournament. The president kept asking me questions about who was there and how I played until, finally, the topic turned to the subject he least liked to discuss: himself.

"The Make a Wish Foundation invited me to the hospital today to meet a ten-year-old boy," he explained. "He is terminally ill . . . and his wish was to meet . . . a president."

His tone was such that he seemed astonished a young boy would choose that as his wish. If the boy had told Make a Wish he wanted to meet *President George Bush* specifically, I knew the president was too sincerely humble to admit that or repeat it to us.

"He has cancer. The little guy was in his hospital bed with tubes and wires," the president continued quietly. "His entire extended family was there in that hospital room. I met each of them during the half-hour I was there."

Bar and I nodded silently and listened.

"That little boy is truly the courageous one. I tried to be as positive and 'presidential' as I could," he explained. "After I said goodbye to everyone, I was walking to the door when I thought I heard the boy say something to me. So I stopped and went back to his bedside and bent down to try to hear him . . . and he just gave me a big, long hug."

A minute passed before he continued his story.

"I barely got out of that room without letting the tears flow."

The three of us seemed to sigh at the same time. I imagined the raw emotion he must have been feeling—the combination of honor and responsibility he felt to bring some measure of happiness to the boy and everyone in the room, but at the same time understanding the pain of the situation. I sensed his sadness and wondered if maybe he'd been reminded of the tragedy he and Bar had endured in 1953 when they lost their nearly four-year-old daughter Robin to leukemia.

"I'd like to ask you two a question," President Bush said to us. "How do you feel about a former president showing emotion? Would it be appropriate to show tears?"

Bar and I looked deeply into his eyes and then at each other. Bar put her hand on his.

"George, emotion shows compassion," Mrs. Bush assured him. "Emotion is real, and your heart is large. People have always been genuinely important to you and I think it's a wonderful thing. Whether you were a president or a father or a brother or a sister, you were part of a very moving moment."

His eyes glistened as the president nodded his head.

In 2013, President Bush wore his heart on his sleeve again when, after meeting a two-year-old boy named Patrick who was stricken with leukemia, the president had his head shaved in solidarity. Members of his Secret Service detail followed suit in support.

It is well known by now that President Bush is an emotional man and his tears try to flow freely. In December 2006, he was giving a speech, which I saw on television and now can watch on YouTube, in front of the Florida Legislature. President Bush spoke about how proud he was of the way his son Jeb handled losing the 1994 Florida governor's race. As his eyes welled and his voice cracked, he pulled out a handkerchief and put it to his face between the choked-up pauses in his speech.

"A true measure of a man is how you handle victory and how you handle defeat . . . he showed with not only words but with actions what decency he had."

When asked later about the speech, the president said, "I don't enjoy breaking up, but when you talk about somebody you love, when you get older, you do it more."

Andy Mill, Olympic Ski Racer, Champion Tournament Fisherman, and TV Host

One year, President Bush and I were among a group of friends fishing for char near the Arctic Circle at Tree River. We had extra high floodwaters that year, which made for very difficult fishing.

In the evening, after a long day fishing along the riverbank, we sat and drank rum and smoked cigars with Ken Raynor, Johnny Morris, and the other fellows on the trip. Most of the time we told fish tales. The president's son, George W. Bush, was serving as president at the time and was, back home, getting some rough press about the Iraq War.

I could tell #41 was a little quiet that day and introspective. All of a sudden, as we sat there, he volunteered to us that it was the negative media coverage of his son bothering him.

"Gosh, it's okay if they criticize me, but when they talk about my children it really hurts." He seemed solemn and introspective, and it was clear his heart was wounded. His sensitive side was visible and animated.

4

YOUR PLACE OR MINE? A WHITE HOUSE WELCOME

My fiancée Anne Forrest and I decided to get married before the 1988 golf season began. After all, my work as a PGA professional kept me busy all summer, and we didn't want to wait until the fall. So Anne picked the date: April 15, 1988, Tax Day!

We only had two days to take a honeymoon after the ceremony, since Cape Arundel was about to open for the season and I needed to be there to welcome the members properly.

Given the time frame, we decided we'd go down to Washington, DC for a couple of days to tour the National Archives and learn about America. We'd become more interested in government and politics during Vice President George H. W. Bush's term since he was a member at Cape Arundel and a friend, so we occasionally got to meet some of the governmental leaders he was involved with or would bring to play golf.

I called around trying to find a hotel room in Washington but was having a hard time, since springtime in DC—when everything is blooming and Congress is in session—is a very busy place. Nevertheless, I didn't want to disappoint Anne, so I brainstormed until I came up with an idea. Maybe there were some hotel rooms kept in reserve for last-minute meetings or governmental purposes? I knew just who might know the answer to that.

I phoned Vice President Bush's secretary, Patty Presock, at his office in Washington.

"By chance does the government have a reserve of rooms in case a dignitary, or a golf professional," I joked, "happens to come in?"

"Hmmm," I heard Patty respond. I'd never asked her for anything, but I certainly didn't want her to stress over it.

"I'm just asking because I'll be coming with my new wife Anne on our honeymoon and am getting shut out of finding a hotel room. I'm not asking for a free room—just for a possible reservation," I explained. "But please don't mention anything to the vice president, though, because I know how he is . . . and so do you."

"Let me check around and call you back," she said.

Within an hour my phone rang and I picked it up.

"Kenny, I hear you're coming to Washington?!"

"Yes, Mr. Vice President, I am . . . but you weren't supposed to know."

"You've got to come and stay with us at the Naval Observatory."

"No, Mr. Bush, thank you, that's very kind of you, but I really didn't mean to impose. I was just checking with Patty about extra hotel rooms. Anne and I are just coming for two days . . ."

"No, no, I insist. We've got a room for you!"

I know I may have been throwing some of the "getaway romance" of a honeymoon to the wind, but how was I to say no to the generous enthusiasm of the vice president? It was final; Anne and I would spend our honeymoon with the Bushes at the vice-presidential residence at the Naval Observatory.

I did, though, eventually muster the courage to tell the vice president no, only a few days later.

Ours had been a small, evening wedding in Kennebunkport on a Friday night with family and very close friends, at South Congregational Church, followed by a reception at a restaurant then called Windows on the Water. We spent our wedding night at Captain Lord Mansion, a quaint, historic sea captain's home that faces the village green—where "Ganny's Garden," dedicated to Mrs. Bush, now grows.

Flash forward about thirty-six hours, and it's about 8:00 a.m. Sunday, and we were hustling to leave for the airport. I carried Anne's suitcase to the car and went back to lock up the house. Just as I had closed and locked the front door, I could hear the phone ringing inside. I quickly set my suitcase down on the porch, pulled my keys out of my pocket, unlocked the door, and clamored into the kitchen. I breathlessly mumbled into the phone, "Hello?"

"Kenny? George Bush."

"Oh, good morning, Mr. Vice President."

"You're coming to Washington today, aren't you?"

"Yes, sir, we are."

"You're coming to stay with us, right?" he asked, sounding excited.

"We are. We're looking forward to it. It's awfully nice of you, sir. We weren't expecting to stay with you . . ."

"You're getting here at about 1:00 or 1:30, right?"

"Yes, sir."

"You want to play golf at about 2:00?"

I took a big breath, steeled myself, and dug deep.

"Well . . . Mr. Vice President . . . I appreciate the invitation, but I'm on my honeymoon," I reminded him. "I think I'd better not play golf."

There was a brief pause, then he asked, "Well, do you mind if I do? Then I'll just see you back at the house afterward later in the evening?"

"Gosh, sir, I sure hope you would play. Don't let us stop you from doing anything. We're just appreciative, and we look forward to seeing you whenever."

"Oh, okay, thanks. I'll go to the course and see you later in the evening."

I thanked him again and, as soon as we hung up, I started hurrying back to the car to drive to the airport and catch our flight. I pulled the front door shut, locked it, turned, and headed down the porch steps when I thought I heard the phone ringing again. "Oh, God," I muttered as I paused on the step, stood still, and listened. Yep—within three beats I heard it. The phone was ringing again.

Anne peered at me out the windshield, tilted her head, and lifted both her palms up as if to ask with a gesture, "What's going on?"

I shrugged and lifted a finger to signal, "One minute." Then I turned and jumped back up the steps and onto the wooden porch, dropped my suitcase, dug through my pocket for the keys, unlocked the door, bounced into the kitchen, and once again, struggling to reach the phone before it stopped ringing, grabbed it off the cradle just in time. It was the vice president calling again!

"Kenny, I thought you said you were getting here between 1:00 and 1:30?"

"We are, sir."

"Well, it's only 8:00 in the morning. Why are you leaving now?"

I couldn't help but chuckle.

"Well, sir, unlike you, we have to find parking in the airport parking lot. We have to wait in line to check our bags. We have to go through security and then make our way to the gate."

"Oh, yeah, okay. I forgot. I'll see you later!"

Ben Wright, Emmy Award–Winning CBS TV Golf Commentator

I became acquainted with Vice President George Bush after playing with him in Cy Laughter's Bogey Busters golf tournament at National Cash Register Club in Dayton, Ohio. We had a very enjoyable game and at the end of the round he gave me his calling card, which included a private telephone number to reach him directly.

"If you're ever in a jam, here I am," Vice President Bush told me as he handed it to me.

A few years later I was experiencing great difficulty in renewing my green card, which would allow me to continue to work for CBS in the United States. After much internal second-guessing as to whether it was appropriate, I decided I had no choice but to ring the number on Bush's card. A humorless, official-sounding man answered the phone, and I meekly gave my name and explained that the vice president had given me the number. The next voice I heard was that of Vice President Bush, greeting me warmly and then listening to my plight.

"Ben, I want you to hold the line," Vice President Bush said. "I'm going to put you on right now with one of my aides and you can rest assured he will make your problem go away."

He did . . . with expedience!

After he became president, the network sent me, with President Bush's permission, to put together a television piece for the CBS Evening News *about his affinity for golf. I went, with a camera crew, to Cape Arundel Golf Club and played a round of golf with the president. On the air, I was gentle in analyzing his swing, which I found to be quick and in need of work. Luckily, later that summer he told me he liked the piece, when, while serving as master of ceremonies, I introduced President Bush to receive the Ambassador of Golf Award at Firestone Country Club, in Akron. Afterward, he invited me to the cottage he was occupying off the sixteenth hole for drinks.*

Later that year, Anne and I, on the television in our living room, watched our honeymoon host, Vice President George Bush, become elected the 41st president of the United States.

And once Vice President Bush and Mrs. Bush became president and first lady in 1989, their generous penchant for sharing and hospitality grew even more evident.

Though I work at Cape Arundel Golf Club all summer, when snow hits Maine we pack up the car and spend some of the winter months in Florida. Mrs. Bush got wind of this and asked my wife Anne, "Where do you stop on your drive down from Maine to Florida?"

Anne explained to the first lady that we just choose any roadside hotel along our East Coast route when we feel like stopping.

"Well, why pay for a hotel? You must come and stay with us at the White House on your way down."

Anne must have looked speechless because Mrs. Bush quickly said, "I insist. You might even find it nicer than a hotel."

So we packed up the car for our stay in Florida. We were new parents with our son Kyle, so we had strollers and playpens and diaper bags and baby formula; since we were headed to the Sunshine State, we had bicycles on the roof and fishing rods sticking out the back window and all the family flotsam and jetsam of a nomadic golf professional jammed into our old Volvo . . . and we were headed for the White House.

During our drive, we had to make calls to the president's secretary so she could keep the Secret Service advised as to where we were and how soon they should expect us to arrive. In late afternoon, after a nine-hour drive from Maine to Washington, DC, we turned off Pennsylvania Avenue, pulled up to the guardhouse of the grand, historic house, and rolled down the window of the cramped, cluttered car.

"We're the Raynors," I said sheepishly to the guard. And then, almost in the inflection of a question rather than a statement, I told him, "We're guests of the president."

Even saying the words was a surreal experience.

"They're expecting you, Mr. Raynor. Welcome to the White House."

Those were words I was happy and humbled to hear.

The next thing we knew, after going through the necessary security procedures, we were driving that Volvo right onto the South Lawn of the White House. They told us to park right next to the door, below the balcony you see on television all the time.

The aura and the majesty of the White House are overwhelming. The sense of place and history, upon walking up to the entrance, gave Anne and me butterflies. But when the door opened up and Mrs. Bush greeted us warmly as friends, the butterflies fluttered away.

The president was, of course, working, but the first lady, with a couple of aides, guided us in. The first room we walked into was kind of an oval-shaped, welcoming room just off the South Lawn. The first hall we then passed through seemed to be lined with security offices and various officials, doctors, and Secret Service people. Then we went up the elevator to the residence level.

What impressed me, initially, was just how beautiful the White House really is. It's full of artifacts, portraits, and artwork depicting our nation's history, but I was also astonished by the beautiful flower arrangements and just how meticulous every person who works there is. The pride they feel working in the White House is amazing. If you were to walk, as I have, into the florist's room when all of the staff are working on the arrangements for a state dinner or into the kitchen, you could just sense the pride and the standard to which the staff aspired: Everything had to be better than perfect. And that's not the standard that the president necessarily sets, but rather, the standard that all of the people who work at the White House set because of the aura of what the building stands for. It's the way it should be—and the way it always has been.

Our arrival had been mind-boggling. Here I was, a golf professional from the state of Maine who happened to have a friend who just became president of the United States. I was overcome by a sense of patriotism and a feeling of pride to be an American. To walk into this monument and to experience it had me asking myself "why me?" Anne and I were fully aware of how blessed we were to have this incredible opportunity.

Mrs. Bush led us to the Lincoln Bedroom and, like any woman might show off her home, she was pointing out items and explaining various things.

"George is very eager to see you and welcome you," Mrs. Bush said. She then let us know where we would meet and what time the president would come up from the Oval Office before letting us get settled in and freshen up.

It was surreal, but when President Bush did come up to the residence at the White House, it had the same feel of any other head of the household coming home from the office (in this case it just happened to be the Oval Office).Once again his greeting made us feel like "family."

Who knows what President Bush dealt with that day, or how many people he spoke to. Did he give any speeches? From where has he flown in? But there we were, with the president, doing exactly what Anne and I would have been doing at home and what millions of other Americans were doing at the same time: sitting back and watching the evening news on television. The difference was that President Bush had the dubious pleasure of being able to watch multiple network newscasts at the same time on multiple screens.

"Mr. President, dinner is served," was the eventual polite announcement of a White House steward.

Mrs. Bush led us into the Jacqueline Kennedy Dining Room.

"Jacqueline Kennedy did such a lovely job renovating and decorating this room," Mrs. Bush said.

The dining room has a fireplace in it and a table that can seat up to eight people. There is a kitchen just off the room as you might expect in any home, except everything you do there has significance. The china we were eating off, for instance, was the Roosevelt china or the Truman china. The teacups we drank out of were presented to the White House by another president. There's nothing that happens there that isn't monumental.

The Bushes were very personable and cordial to the waiters who served the meal. They expressed their appreciation throughout dinner each time even a water glass was refilled. The Bushes embraced the stewards as part of the family. The feedback we sensed was that everyone who worked in the White House loved serving the Bushes because the Bushes made them feel so appreciated.

The modus operandi of the Bush Family, whether you were visiting them at the White House during his presidency, or the Naval Observatory during his vice presidency, or at their Walker's Point home in Kennebunkport, is to always get a little exercise after dinner.

"Hey, it's a beautiful evening. Let's take a walk around the South Lawn," the president suggested. (If it were Walker's Point, he would have suggested walking down to the gate; there's a track at the Naval Observatory.) What that basically meant was "the party's over and we're going to bed after the walk. You're free to do what you want."

Sure it's diplomatic, but in fact it's a wonderful way to conclude a very special day.

As we walked down to get to the lawn, Mrs. Bush would pop in to the Blue Room or the Red Room or the China Room or the library and show us items of interest.

"Have you seen this, Kenny?" she would ask. Or, "Anne, can I show you something?"

I presumed Mrs. Bush had done this many times, but she seemed very enthusiastic about sharing the house and every detail in it with us!

Once we got outside for some fresh air and had a peaceful walk around the South Lawn, we decided to check out the White House putting green. It was dark by then, and the Secret Service agents walked with us, so people on the other side of the fence couldn't even tell it was the president.

After the walk, and after the Bushes went to bed, Anne and I went back to the China Room to linger a little longer and look more at things. We were in awe. We could go anywhere we wanted as guests of the president, so we peeked into the State Dining Room, the ballroom, and everything else.

Even though we were on our own in the White House, the Secret Service agents did not follow us, but there were stewards in different areas and agents at different posts . . . and they knew where we were. The residence level is the first couple's living space, but guests like us stay there also, in the other bedrooms just down the hall—but it's a big hall. The White House is a big building, after all.

Paula Poundstone, comedian and first woman ever to emcee the White House Correspondents Dinner

I'd made it very clear I was a Democrat. So on the day I was to emcee the typically irreverent White House Correspondents Dinner and I was told President Bush had extended an invitation for me to visit him at the White House, I presumed this invitation was only presented so he could censor me by instructing me as to what kind of jokes he felt I could tell that night and what areas he considered to be inappropriate or "off-limits." So I went to the White House "loaded for bear" and ready to defend my right to free speech.

During my visit, I found President Bush to be charming and friendly as he gave me a personal tour of the Oval Office.

I finally asked him, "Okay, what areas do you not want me to joke about tonight?"

President Bush just looked at me and smiled before he answered, "Aw, Paula, you can say anything you want tonight!"

He could not have been kinder.

Maybe he had it set up ahead of time with his aides that if he "got bored of Paula Poundstone" he should be interrupted with an "urgent phone call," but that's exactly what happened. One of the president's assistants came in saying that Russian president Boris Yeltsin was on the line calling for him. He apologized and graciously excused himself as I yielded to Yeltsin.

Eventually it was time for bed. It was hard to believe, but we were about to spend our first visit to the White House in the famed Lincoln Bedroom—on the second floor in the southeast corner of the building. We learned the room was not originally a bedroom, but rather, a working office for President Lincoln, who met there with his Cabinet members, as did presidents before him. The sprawling bed—which Mary Todd Lincoln likely bought but her husband probably never slept in—has a massive headboard.

President Lincoln signed the Gettysburg Address in the room, and a holograph copy, one of only five signed, dated, and titled by Lincoln, is displayed on the desk.

There are two rooms in the Lincoln Bedroom, including the Lincoln Sitting Room. The warm welcome and thoughtfulness of the White House staff was evident: They had a babysitter and crib all set up in advance for our son Kyle, who was about nine months old, and making the first trip of his life . . . it just happened to be to the White House! We had a photo snapped with Kyle and the president, and Kyle must have been inspired that day. It was on that day that little Kyle let go of our hands and took his very first steps . . . right there in the Lincoln Bedroom!

The year prior on a March afternoon our son Kyle had been born at Maine Medical Center, in Portland. The hospital switchboard operator was beside himself that day. The White House operator was calling.

"The president of the United States would like to be connected to Kyle Raynor, please," is what he heard—once he could believe he'd actually heard it! Needless to say the switchboard operator at Maine Medical Center doesn't get calls like that every day, if ever! So he was trying to do his best to connect the White House operator to Kyle Raynor but having no luck locating a hospital room with a patient by that name. He was frantic. The president of the United States was calling, and he didn't want to keep him waiting! They finally put two-and-two together and figured out the person the president wanted to be connected to, Kyle Raynor, was only about four hours old!

"Sir, Kyle Raynor is a newborn," the hospital switchboard operator told the White House operator.

"Oh the president—he got me again," said the White House operator, laughing.

When President Bush was finally connected and came on the line in Anne's room, he was laughing too, knowing that he'd caused this problem with everyone looking for Kyle Raynor.

He congratulated Anne for bringing a beautiful child into the world.

Not long after we got our newborn home from the hospital, Kyle Raynor got an envelope addressed to him—the first he'd ever received in the US mail—from the president of the United States. Inside was an eight-by-ten photo of President Bush which now hangs, framed, on the wall outside the door of the bedroom Kyle grew up in. The photo was a rugged, close-up profile of the president wearing a Navy flight jacket with the presidential seal over a dark blue cardigan sweater with a lobster pin on it. The photo was clearly taken on the seaside rocks at Kennebunkport, but the hand-signed autograph in the top border read: "March 16, 1990 — signed at Camp David."

Below the photo, which was captioned in script font simply "The President," the handwriting continued:

Dear Kyle,
Welcome to this exciting world. You're a lucky guy because you have a wonderful Mom and Dad. When you get bigger I want you to go fishing with me. Barbara and I love you already.
Good luck, big guy!
George Bush.

Naturally the "big guy" was up first, and early, as we awakened in the White House.

Had it all been a dream?

After all, during his four years in the White House, the president and Mrs. Bush welcomed only 273 people for overnight stays in the Lincoln Bedroom. That list included Bob Hope, Johnny Carson, Reverend Billy Graham, Ted Williams, Crystal Gayle, Lee Greenwood, Don Johnson, Dana Carvey, the Oak Ridge Boys, and . . . the Raynors.

We knew it wasn't just a dream when, on the doorknob of the Lincoln Bedroom, we found a hanging menu offering us choices for breakfast and options as to where we'd like it to be served. It could be served in the bedroom, or in the dining room, or on the upper floor in the solarium.

We tried to make ourselves as inconspicuous as possible. We wanted to pick the place that was easiest for the staff to serve us breakfast, especially since we had a baby.

We loved the solarium, though, because it was a fun room. It was like a casual TV room in anyone else's house. There was even a little refrigerator with some drinks and sodas and lemonades in it. You can relax up there without bothering anyone. Just down the hall was a pool table. I made sure to shoot a rack of pool just to be able to say "I shot a rack of pool at the White House." As we relaxed at breakfast on our own in the solarium, we looked out the window overlooking the Washington Monument and it reminded us that we were actually in the White House! We figuratively pinched ourselves.

An hour later, my friend the president could have been speaking to a crowd of two thousand or to a world leader on the phone or behind closed doors in the Situation Room. He could have been anywhere via motorcade, *Marine One*, or *Air Force One*. We were, by then, back in the packed-up Volvo, just a few miles down the road by car — destined, that night, for a pizza in a roadside motel instead of dinner with the president and a snooze in a White House bedroom.

That was our only stay in the Lincoln Bedroom, but we were fortunate to be invited back to stay overnight in the White House on a number of other occasions. We became more comfortable, but no less awed, with each additional visit. I got so comfortable that on one occasion I woke up early, just after dawn, and decided it might be fun to take a swim in the White House pool. It's a simple, outdoor pool over by the Oval Office, and at that hour it was very quiet, so I dove in and swam some laps. I was just kind of dog-paddling around and enjoying the setting and the novelty of it when I suddenly heard a voice. It was President Bush.

"Ahoy! Who is the 'great white whale' in the pool?" he cried out.

He was making his way to work at 7:00 a.m. sharp in the Oval Office, with the Secret Service in tow, and the weight of the world on his shoulders, but he had time to send a parting shot at me in this swimming pool!

During one of our other visits, we happened to be staying in the White House on Halloween night. The president and Mrs. Bush invited us to overnight in the Queen's Room. True to form, after a wonderful dinner, Mrs. Bush suggested, "It's a beautiful night. Let's take a walk around . . . and then we're off to bed."

Before we headed down to walk outside, Mrs. Bush excused herself for a moment and President Bush said to my wife, "Annie, it is a little cold tonight. Do you need a coat?"

When Anne said she'd appreciate a jacket, she was surprised to then hear him ask, "What kind of coat would you like?"

"Oh whatever you grab, sir, will be fine thank you," Anne answered.

"Gimme just a minute," President Bush said, disappearing around the corner for a moment.

Being from New England, Anne smiled when he emerged with a Boston Red Sox jacket and placed it over her shoulders.

It could just as easily have been a New England Patriots coat or a Boston Celtics or Bruins jacket, because that was the night we learned that when you're president of the United States you have, in your collection and at your disposal, coats from practically every sports team in America.

President Bush, Anne, and I found ourselves waiting for Mrs. Bush while standing with a White House steward who would take us down in the elevator to ground level for our walk.

"Bar," the president yelled out, "Where are ya? Where are ya?"

A woman then came out of the president's residence bedroom calling out, "Has anybody seen Barbara Bush? Anyone know where Barbara Bush is?"

The woman was the first lady herself, wearing a rubber Barbara Bush Halloween mask!

The steward was laughing hysterically, as was President Bush, at the sight of the real Barbara Bush wearing a Barbara Bush mask in the White House residence!

Anne and I were grinning from ear to ear as she kept the mask on and we rode down in the elevator. Mrs. Bush walked directly to the Secret Service office and called out again, "Anybody seen Barbara Bush?"

With everyone laughing President Bush asked her, "Are you ever going to take that mask off?"

After Anne and I had received the courtesies of the Bushes at the Naval Observatory during the vice presidency, had spent overnights at the White House on a number of occasions, and had attended cocktail parties, lunches, and dinners at the Bushes' home on Walker's Point, there was only one thing left to do—return the hospitality. So it was that in April 1992 we decided to invite the president of the United States and the first lady for dinner at our home in Kennebunkport.

In a way, inviting them to dinner was like asking a pretty girl who doesn't get asked out on dates: many people are afraid to because they think they'll be rejected. I didn't want to be one of those people.

Eventually I floated the idea briefly to the president while we were on the golf course. He seemed to like the idea, so I followed up a few days later by calling the president's secretary Patty. She knew of my relationship with President Bush, and she always made me feel important throughout his presidency.

"Ken, hang on, I know he'd love to talk to you," she would often say when I had only phoned to speak to her about a detail. I hadn't asked for him, but regardless of what the president was doing I got the sense from her she thought my call was important because I was a friend. She knew it would make him feel good to talk to a friend about golf or fishing just for a moment in the middle of his day, knowing the type of day he was having.

Ultimately, I reiterated the dinner invitation, more formally, to Patty, who repeated the invitation to President and Mrs. Bush.

And guess what?

They accepted, and would come to dinner when they visited Kennebunkport for Easter, on April 17, 1992.

Of course, that means other people get involved. His staff has to know his movements and whereabouts. It was standard procedure that security officers came days ahead to examine our property and know the surroundings. They walked all over the yard and brought the canine unit out. For added safety, we didn't tell the neighbors about the scheduled dinner. No one knew anything about what was to transpire.

Then there was the task of setting the menu. We had a feeling for what the Bushes enjoyed — we knew he liked portabella mushrooms and did not like broccoli, for example. In fact, the whole world knew he didn't like broccoli, because he very publicly said so, in March of 1990, when he held a press conference outside the White House and was asked about a "broccoli ban" he instilled on *Air Force One*.

"I do not like broccoli and I haven't liked it since I was a little kid and my mother made me eat it," he insisted. "And I'm president of the United States, and I'm not going to eat any more broccoli!"

Washington being Washington, ten tons of broccoli florets were delivered in trucks by a California broccoli farmers association in protest.

We, though, were thrilled to share our broccoli-free home with the Bushes.

(*White House photo/Susan Biddle*)

We live in a two-level, comfortable home we built on a beautiful, rural, tree-lined piece of rolling land about five miles from Walker's Point, which is on the ocean. When the day came, we made certain the house was clean. We'd invited Anne's younger brother Bill Forrest to join us, and our son Kyle was two years old at the time.

Anne and I were waiting on the front porch when President and Mrs. Bush emerged from the vehicle, and the strobe of flashbulbs lit the night as I shook his hand and welcomed him. Despite the photo-taking entourage, personal aides, and Secret Service agents, this was not a state visit. He was not coming as POTUS, after all. He was coming as a friend—and he made that point clear by pulling a fishing rod out of the limousine as a gift to me.

The relaxed, casual dinner turned into a tradition that has lasted for years. And each year the president won't let us change the menu from the original visit:

Portabella mushrooms
Anne's cauliflower casserole
Oysters on the half-shell
Cheese-stuffed, twice-baked potato
Baked, stuffed tomatoes
Marinated flank steak

The president says, "It's my favorite meal of the year. Why would we ever change it?"

Get-togethers with the Bushes didn't happen every day. They didn't happen every week. They didn't happen every month. But every time we were blessed to be involved with the Bushes, we were careful to stay in the moment and appreciate it—whether we were at their place or ours.

5

A THOUSAND PUTTS OF LIGHT

I t's been written that I've played more golf with presidents of the United States than any PGA professional in history. Most of those were by the invitation of President George H. W. Bush over our thirty-plus-year friendship. Some were with his son, President George W. Bush, and, since he's been out of office, I've occasionally enjoyed playing with the "presidential twosome" alongside friends. I've also enjoyed a few rounds with President Bill Clinton when he came to visit President Bush. Over the course of these rounds, I've come to understand the importance of relaxation for these leaders, who are forced to endure such a high level of stress on a daily basis. Thus, it has been quite an experience watching commanders-in-chief relax through golf and other pursuits.

I have spent many days on the golf course or in fishing boats with President George H. W. Bush. We'd fish locally on the Atlantic Ocean or just in the Kennebunk River, a tributary that separates our town of Kennebunkport from Kennebunk. For ten years after the president was out of office, we'd travel to Labrador in pursuit of the elusive Atlantic salmon and on a few occasions traveled to the Arctic Circle pursuing Arctic char of world-record size. Multiple days were spent on the golf course when sometimes it would be just the two of us. We might go out and play a quick nine holes or just spend some time chipping and putting when he had a busier schedule. President Bush might do a little putting on the practice green or maybe even cast off the riverbank because it was too choppy to go out to sea.

The golf course and club was a location of serenity for President Bush and a spot for relaxation and enjoyment. It wasn't always about coming to play eighteen holes. Sometimes, he'd just drop by to say hello or he might check to see what was in his locker — just because. He loved just being in the place where his family and friends have played.

Other times he'd duck in to do his Christmas shopping for his staff in the golf shop. He would pick out each gift himself. He'd have a list of everyone on his staff and their sizes and would select shirts and other items. We'd wrap the items up and ship them down to the staff in Houston or get them over to the Walker's Point house. President Bush would give the shop manager Heather a quick hug and brighten everyone's day.

> **Steve Elkington, PGA Tour Player and Major Championship Winner**
> *President Bush came to Australia for the 1998 President's Cup matches when my fellow Aussie Greg Norman and I were able to beat Fred Couples and Davis Love 2–1 in the afternoon four-ball. Couples and Love were the best pairing the American team had. President Bush came in and was gracious to us, even though Couples and Love were both friends of his. The president came in and tipped his hat to us, which was very nice.*

Sometimes we played with Gen. Brent Scowcroft, who had been President Bush's national security advisor and had served the same role under President Ford.

The president phoned me on one of those days.

"Kenny, why don't you come down to the house? I have something you might like to see. I gave a speech and someone there gave me a beautiful new fishing rod as a gift," he said. "Why don't you come on over and we can have a quick lunch and set up the rod to catch the big one?"

"Sounds great, Mr. President. I'll be over right after I finish giving my morning lessons."

I got to Walker's Point and the two of us sat down and had a quality lunch talking about fishing and friends, but quickly the topic changed to the president's new gift. He was like a kid on Christmas morning. There is a closet by his bedroom that contains a lot of sports items he's been presented with over time. Some of the items are as simple as a dozen golf balls with a logo on them or a fishing reel, or something for tennis or running, but they're all fun gifts sent from different organizations and individuals. He was showing me a few items when I noticed something on the back shelf, so I reached for it and pulled it out.

"What's this?" I asked.

"It's an exploding golf ball," he said. But then the light of battle came into his eyes. "Take that and put it in your pocket. You've got to get that on the tee when we play golf later with Brent Scowcroft!"

General Scowcroft was always known for using old, yellowed, discolored golf balls. "Manila-colored," is the way President Bush described them, like a manila envelope.

An hour or so later, on the first tee, President Bush was watching, like a bad school kid, waiting to see this practical joke played on his national security advisor—right in front of the world's press, which had assembled near the first tee, as they usually did, when the sitting president came to play golf.

Scowcroft hit his opening tee shot, and it wasn't very good.

It was our chance, so President Bush and I simultaneously, and probably a touch too enthusiastically, called out to Scowcroft "Hit another one, Brent. Forget that one. Hit till you're happy to go ahead."

"I'll even give you room service and tee up a brand new ball for you," I insisted, putting the trick ball on the tee at Scowcroft's feet. "Hit a good one, general."

The president was over with the media members, looking like an orchestra conductor, making sure their eyes, and cameras, were pointed at Scowcroft.

Scowcroft took a big swing and when his club head made contact with the ball it exploded into a cloud of dust. The president was laughing hysterically and within hours some of the late night talk shows aired the video clip. It was great for the game of golf to see the president enjoying the game with his friends.

It took a while for Scowcroft to seek revenge on the president for the prank, but when he finally did, it was with style. About a year later, Anne and I were having dinner with another couple at the White Barn, a very nice local restaurant, and when it came time to order, we were talking about President Bush's publicly acknowledged dislike for broccoli. The waitress had overheard some of our conversation.

"Excuse me, but I love to crochet and knit. If you like, I could knit a set of golf head covers which would look like they had broccoli florets growing out of the tops," she offered. As you might imagine, we accepted her offer to create the head covers, which we subsequently delivered to Scowcroft.

Scowcroft wasted no time and once again on the first tee in front of the press, he made an eloquent speech touting the health values and deliciousness of broccoli. As a bemused President Bush looked on and listened, Scowcroft concluded his speech by presenting President Bush with the head covers of his least favorite vegetable! Being a good sport, President Bush kept them on his clubs for the rest of the season. Now they remain on display at the George H. W. Bush Presidential Library in College Station, Texas.

The president struck back again, though, with a round of golf, which he and General Scowcroft were scheduled to play at the famed Mid-Ocean Club in Bermuda. Mid-Ocean Club is a classic example of a golden-era golf course. Charles Blair Macdonald designed and built the hilly, rolling golf course in 1921. It would be redundant to describe it as "ocean-side" because everything on the slender islands of Bermuda is ocean-side. But a few of the holes play, in part, right along the ocean.

The trouble was the president and General Scowcroft were scheduled to play Mid-Ocean during an oncoming hurricane. There were forty-mile-per-hour winds and multiple inches of rain.

Shortly after their trip I saw General Scowcroft at Cape Arundel Golf Club.

"How was your round at Mid-Ocean Club?"

"Ken, I thought I was going to drown in the middle of the fairway," he answered. "It was raining sideways, but President Bush was wondering whether to hit 7-iron or 6-iron as if it were sunny!"

With the wind that was coming across that island poor Brent Scowcroft, who only weighs about 150 pounds soaking wet, could have been blown right off of the second tee or from atop the hill on the fifth hole.

"I have never been so soaking wet in my entire life," Scowcroft told me. "But he never considered not playing. Not for one single second."

Jack Nicklaus, Winner of More Major Championships Than Any Other Golfer in History

Former President Bush has been so respectful and incredibly supportive of anything and everything my wife Barbara and I have ever done. He is a long-time member of the Memorial Tournament's Captains Club. He has been to the Memorial Tournament and remained supportive throughout the years.

He and his wife Barbara have been great friends for many years, and my Barbara and I cherish the relationship we are fortunate to have with them. You might say that President Bush is from the old school of dealing with friends, and I have probably received twenty or more handwritten notes from him over the years.

President Bush has always loved the game of golf, although he will display a self-deprecating humor when describing his game. But there is no questioning his love and passion for it. And as a golfer, President Bush plays golf the way it should be played — fast. If everyone played golf as fast as former president Bush did, we wouldn't have some of the problems we have today in the game. ☺

On the final day of the 1998 Presidents Cup at Royal Melbourne, President Bush had come to Australia to support the event, and he stood on the first tee to greet every player before their singles matches. It was mid-December, which can mean unpredictable weather in Melbourne. From the first pairing until the last, the temperature must have dropped 40 degrees — and with that a steady rain blew in. President Bush never left the tee or even flinched. He stood in the pouring rain and greeted every player who teed off that final day, and did so with grace and a big smile. It might have been a small gesture to him, but to me, it spoke volumes about the person he is and his character.

President Bush would not be what some might expect of someone who is so much in the public eye and has served as the commander-in-chief. He's a very thoughtful, caring, and considerate person.

I understood what had happened. President Bush chose his "moments" very well. With the pressures of the office, President Bush had to make effective use of his time to find moments of relaxation. If he found two hours in his heavy schedule to break away from the powers of his office and get away from the pressure, he was going to do it — even if it was during a hurricane or monsoon.

The good news is President Bush did make it back to Bermuda on a later trip with his friends Jim Nantz, Paul Marchand, and Tom Kelley in much better weather. President Bush was so excited he brought four matching light-blue golf shirts for them to wear on the golf course — like a little team going out to play. He loved that type of gentle gesture and often engaged in playful acts of lighthearted fun just like that to keep things in perspective.

I think that method of keeping a balance in his life helped him make good decisions because his mind was not clouded. President Bush always seemed to focus on the activity at hand. In some cases, that activity was golf. Sometimes it was fishing. But then when he went back to the big, important decisions, he was clearer because of his downtime.

But sometimes, the pursuit of golf is not only used as a stress relief. Other times, it serves as a means by which the president and others can support important causes.

One example is the president's participation in an event casually called "The Pike," which is an annual charity tournament that began as The Gary Pike Tournament to raise funds for Gary's House at Portland Mercy Hospital. Gary's House is named for Gary Pike, an engaging, courageous eighteen-year-old who lost his life to cancer in 1991 after a two-year battle during which his family suffered financial hardship to support him. The house offers accommodations for families of loved ones fighting serious illness or receiving treatment.

Early on, the golf tournament and gala received the support of President and Mrs. Bush, who donated auction items, participated in the tournament, and still continue to make appearances when they can. The president, knowing that he would not always be able to participate, allowed us to call it the George H. W. Bush Cape Arundel Celebrity Golf Classic at Cape Arundel, hoping his name would help bring in more donations.

The President's Pike Point of Light Award is presented each year at the tournament gala. The award, originally given by President Bush during each day of his presidency, is now awarded by a nonprofit foundation he founded to people anywhere in America who participate meaningfully in volunteer service and are making a difference in the community.

President Bush used the phrase "a thousand points of light" during his memorable acceptance speech at the 1988 Republican National Convention. From the podium in New Orleans, before the balloons fell, the then–vice president described volunteer organizations as "a brilliant diversity spread like stars; like a thousand points of light in a broad and peaceful sky."

As the crowds cheered their presidential nominee, Vice President Bush also promised to "Keep America moving forward, always forward, for a better America, for an endless enduring dream and a thousand points of light."

The tournament has evolved since its inception in 2002. For instance, celebrities were invited and enlisted for the participants to play golf with, including former president Bill Clinton and New England Patriots quarterbacks Tom Brady and Steve Grogan, both of whom played in Super Bowls.

Boston Bruins hockey legend Derek Sanderson, Red Sox pitchers Luis Tiant and Curt Schilling, Fox News host Greta Van Susteren, former PGA Tour commissioner Deane Beman, speed skater Bonnie Blair, and CBS sportscaster Jim Nantz—who emceed the gala event a number of times and has become a friend of the president through the years—are among the notables who have come help light it up.

Jim Nantz, Emmy Award–Winning CBS Sports PGA Tour, NFL, and NCAA Anchor

President Bush is never going to ask you for a favor. He does not want to be treated with any specialness even though he was leader of the free world. He is the least entitled person I have ever met.

If you go into a restaurant, he is going to make sure you are going to sit in the best seat, with your back to the wall, looking over the entire restaurant. Watch a group of eight people stroll into your local restaurant and head to the round table in the corner. Notice how the first person always walks all the way around the table and takes the back chair so they can take in the whole span of the restaurant and sit there in the "Godfather seat." It's human nature. But President Bush never felt entitled to the best seat and the best view. He wanted others to feel comfortable . . . and he would settle into what was left over.

Even getting into a car with him — which has happened for me on literally hundreds of occasions — he's never going to try to take the best seat in the car even though he should. In the Chevy Suburbans he's driven in there is a third row in the back. When everyone approaches the vehicles, guess who was fighting to awkwardly have to step over the pulled-back bucket seat in order to climb into the very back row?

Eighty-year-old George Bush.

Travel with a group and watch how most people angle to get the front seat. If President Bush is going to fight you for anything, he's going to fight you for that worst seat. He wants you to be comfortable.

Nantz's participation in the tournament was a definite draw to the fundraiser, but it also gave him a chance to visit his dear friend President Bush. In fact, Jim has said he'd rather play golf with President Bush than anyone else in the world. That's a big statement given the worldwide connections he has and the locations he's capable of visiting. It tells me it's not all about the golf; it's about the experience. I think the president is extremely good at creating a memorable experience no matter what you're doing. Whether it was a fishing trip or a golf outing, the president, standing on the first tee, would tell me, "You learn a lot about a guy playing eighteen holes or standing in a river with him all day in your waders casting side by side."

He's so right. Think about how a guy reacts when he misses a three-foot putt. What does he do when he's hitting good shots? Is it different than when he's hitting terrible shots and losing balls?

How's he doing when casting? Or losing a big fish? Or when he's simply not catching any fish? It's not all about the "catch." It's about the atmosphere and the experience. Have a look at the cliffs and the birds and the sky. Look around at the beautiful river and the fjord.

"Who needs fish when you have good friends?" is the way the president once autographed a photo of us fishing together in the Kennebunk River.

Once Jim told me about the day that he and the president played their first round of golf together, it came as no surprise to me how quickly their friendship developed and that they've been such supportive friends over the course of many years. It was 1993, and #41 had been just out of office for a couple of months. Paul Marchand, who was the head golf professional at Houston Country Club and was a friend of Nantz and President Bush, received a request from the president asking to be introduced to Nantz.

"Paul, I'd like to meet Jim Nantz because he's a Houstonian (Jim went to the University of Houston) and he's broadcasting sporting events," the president told Marchand. So Paul, knowing how much he loved sports, arranged a meeting and a round of golf at Memorial Park Golf Club, in Houston. Nantz, for his part, was honored the president had an awareness that a kid from The University of Houston had made it to the network.

On the day they'd arranged, Nantz and Marchand arrived at Memorial Park early and were waiting in the clubhouse when the motorcade arrived. Nantz remembers President Bush jumping out and extending a warm handshake before heading into the pro shop to check in for the round. Nantz and Marchand followed him in.

"Hey, I want to pay for four green fees, and two golf carts and two additional golf carts for my security agents," President Bush told the golf staff attendant behind the desk.

"Oh, no, no, Mr. President. No, no, no; you're our guest," the attendant answered.

At that point President Bush put his wallet right down on the counter and said, "I insist."

"No, no, Mr. President. We insist. You're our guest."

Typical of how President Bush handles things with such grace, he replied, "You don't understand. I don't want you to think that I came here looking to play golf for free. That's not right. So please let me pay for the four green fees and the four golf carts? Because if I don't, I probably will never come back because I'm afraid you're going to think that I think I can come out here anytime I like for free and I don't like the sound of that. So please let me pay so I will be able to come back again sometime."

This arm-twisting exercise went on for three or four minutes and finally, the attendant said, "Okay, Mr. President. The fees and charges are $240.00."

The president pulled out a credit card and off they went.

Thus was the start of many golf outings in which both Jim and the president participated. So when it came time for our charity fundraiser in 2000, Jim was able to bring fourteen-time PGA Tournament winner Ken Venturi into the mix.

Venturi came back to the George H. W. Bush Celebrity Pro-Am for Gary's House at Cape Arundel for a number of years, including his last year on the air at CBS (2002).

In fact, Venturi came to Kennebunkport for our pro-am the very day after his retirement, which concluded a thirty-five-year career on television. Just as he'd done the day before to conclude his career, Ken gave a goodbye of sorts and recounted some of the highlights of his time in golf and television. Being in that room that night and being part of that scene was probably one of my career highlights as a lover of the game of golf and its traditions and what it stands for. The camaraderie was palpable, and understanding the passion that Ken and Jim had for each other and the passion that Ken had for golf and life was very moving. Ken Venturi, who often welled up, spoke from the heart.

In July 1989, a colorful player from professional golf's past, Doug Sanders, a fun-loving southerner who was active in Houston, came to play with President Bush—who started his career in the Texas oil business and still spends half of each year in Houston. I played with Sanders, Bucky Bush (the president's brother), and President Bush at Cape Arundel. From across the golf course you could always spot Sanders in a foursome because he was known for his colorful, flamboyant clothing. He must have hundreds of pairs of shoes to match every shade of clothing imaginable. He was a real "Dapper Dan."

If you're going to dress like that, you'd better have the game to back it up. And Sanders did. He won twenty times on tour between 1956 and 1972, and lost the 1970 British Open in a playoff at St. Andrews after pushing a three-foot putt which would have won him the championship on the last hole of regulation. But he definitely won the PGA Tour personality contest every time. Women loved him. And men admired him.

On this July day, Sanders wore lavender trousers and a light, multicolored, patterned sweater with matching purple saddle-style shoes that pulled together all of the colors. The rest of us looked drab in our traditional khaki, olive green, gray, and fawn-colored, solid, muted, monochromatic golf clothing.

Sanders was regaling us with stories from the PGA Tour, and at the second hole, trying to hit a draw around the tree and down the dogleg, he snap-hooked a terrible tee shot instead down into the marsh.

"That's the problem now that I've gotten older," Sanders announced to the group. "In my heyday I used to hit a little, soft fade down the middle of every fairway . . . and I'd hook at night. Now I'm hooking during the day and fading at night!"

The president got a big kick out of that.

When we reached the seventeenth green, we decided to have a photograph taken before things got busy at the end of the round. The president was in office at the time, so there would be a crowd of reporters and others waiting for him at the eighteenth green and when we got back to the clubhouse. Sanders didn't want the standard "stare into the camera mug shot line-up," though. He wanted an "action shot." He had an idea . . . and he went to work on it like a Hollywood director.

Sanders took two tees and stuck them into the side walls of the hole to create a little "bridge" across, but hidden just below, the top edge. He sat the ball down on the tees, so it looked like the ball was tumbling into the hole.

Ken Raynor, Bucky Bush, President Bush, and Doug Sanders playfully "fake" an "action shot." The putt appears to be falling but the ball was actually placed on two tees suspended over the hole.
(*White House photo/David Valdez*)

Then he had President Bush grab his long Pole-Kat putter about eight feet from the hole and pose with it as if he'd just putted the ball and was holding his finish to see if it went in.

Sanders had the White House photographer, who always follows the president, snap the photo just as Sanders staged Bucky and me to raise our fists and jump into the air as if we were rejoicing to see the putt go in! Sanders posed cheering, too. It looked like a candid action shot snapped just as the ball fell into the hole.

It's amazing what grown men will do to amuse themselves, eh?

Dottie Pepper, LPGA Seventeen-Time Winner and TV Golf Commentator
I did make the late August trip but I did not break the course record! However, during the round, the president came the closest he ever did to making a hole in one. His shot was not more than two inches away from the hole. To this day he has never had a hole in one. His son Marvin reminded me of that when I ran into him in Washington, DC earlier this year, but Marvin said the president still prides himself on that ever-so-close one!

The president had other notable friends come to visit him and to play at Cape Arundel, too. One year PGA Tour player Brad Faxon, a New Englander, came to play with President Bush. Brad was playing okay. He was consistent, but not shooting super low numbers. We were playing along in and out of rain showers and he was about four-under-par so it didn't look like the record of 62 (seven-under-par) was in jeopardy. Suddenly, when Faxon made a birdie on the sixteenth hole the record was in range. If he birdied the seventeenth and made par on the eighteenth hole, he would shoot 61!

Faxon hit a great drive off the tee on the 365-yard, par-4 seventeenth hole. His approach shot left him a fairly close putt for birdie, which he was lining up when he noticed President Bush holding an umbrella over his head to shield Faxon from the rain.

"I began to feel how important my chance to break the record was to the president," Faxon told me later.

Mind you, Faxon won eight times on the PGA Tour—where he set records for putting proficiency—and was a two-time Ryder Cup player in addition to

GEORGE BUSH

June 27, 2000

Dear Dottie,

Pete Roussel tells us that you might be able to come to Kennebunkport for a couple of days. "Great Tidings of Joy!"

How about this idea? Come up here on Monday August 28th -- spend Monday and Tuesday nights with us here on Walker's Point, leaving on Wednesday August 30th.

Here's the plan. I firmly believe you can beat Freddie Couples' course record of 62. The record did survive challenges from Irwin, Palmer, Olazaball, and Love to name but a few. It even survived about 6 challenges from our friend Jim Nantz. (Nantz, Couples & Love will be trying again in July). But here's why I think you can do it.

Davis Love, a Pepper fan, told me at lunch yesterday in Sea Island that he felt with your short game you could do it. You see the course is not long – par 69 with one five par and that will be a birdie hole for you for sure. That's the only hole where you'll use a fairway wood (or metal).

We will not have "show biz" golf – no ropes, no fans. It will be family. I will have had a new hip put in by then so I fully expect that the "Ranking Committee" will let me make the cut to play with you. Same for Barbara. We will both be at the Open on July 28th – discuss then?

You do not have to play golf all the time. No! We will fish, rest, have massages, lobsters, fast boat, backgammon, puzzle making – all in all you will be treated as family – like it or not.

Say "Yes". Pretty please – "Say Yes".

Sincerely,

WALKER'S POINT, POST OFFICE BOX 492, KENNEBUNKPORT, MAINE 04046
PHONE (207) 967-5800 / FAX (207) 967-0255

his many amateur titles. Setting the Cape Arundel Golf Club course record wasn't high on his list of goals, but suddenly, with the president of the United States holding the umbrella for him, Faxon was feeling it.

He made the nice birdie putt on the seventeenth, and so he needed a simple par on the eighteenth to break the record. We were all excited to be a part of it, and no one more than President Bush.

Everyone knew what was at stake. The eighteenth is a simple hole, and Faxon, under the pressure, hit a fine drive that went all the way over the driveway that crosses the fairway, leaving him a little flip-wedge or less into the green. He hit his second shot — the pitch shot — right at the hole but it was a little long and, with the weather having put a film of water on his clubface, the ball didn't bite and hold near the hole. It rolled to the back of the green.

The hole was in the front of the green, so Faxon went up to the back and putted his ball back down the slope toward the hole. He's one of the greatest putters ever to have lived, so he almost holed the putt to shoot 60!

Once again President Bush was holding the umbrella for Faxon, and now he's pacing back and forth, examining the little putt he has left for par, reading the break.

"I was nervous over that three-foot putt because I know President Bush wanted to see the record broken," Faxon admitted.

He finally hit the putt and the ball rolled toward the hole . . . and lipped out. Another 62 — no course record.

He had 61 in his pocket but failed to make par. We were all shocked.

We had dinner with Faxon that evening at the president's house. Brad was disappointed, but that didn't stop the Bush Family from bringing out the famous "needle" and teasing him about his eighteenth-hole gaffe.

Brad Faxon, PGA Tour Player

The first time I met President Bush he was just out of office and playing in the AT&T National Pro-Am at Pebble Beach with Hale Irwin. Their pro-am didn't make the cut, but for Sunday's final round, playing with my father Brad, I got paired with Irwin, who'd made the professional cut. While we were playing the fourth hole, we noticed three black limousines driving down the cart path at Pebble Beach, which was a very unusual site. Out hopped the president and Mrs. Bush!

Anytime you meet a president (especially one who you respect and admire), you get nervous and excited, even if you're a PGA Tour player. The president and Mrs. Bush walked with us inside the ropes, watching us play, and on the very first hole they saw my dad sink a fifty-footer across the green.

"Brad, you're my favorite golfer I have ever met," Barbara Bush told my father with her arm around him. It was a moment he'd never forget!

Sometime later, at a Massachusetts Golf Association banquet, I met President Bush again. He was being presented with the Francis Ouimet Award for Lifetime Contributions to Golf. My grandfather, at ninety-three, was also being honored, since he'd given the largest donation ever to the Francis Ouimet Scholarship Fund. President Bush loved my grandfather's speech, and I presented the president with a duplicate of the putter I use on tour with my name on it.

"Why don't you and your wife Dory come visit us this summer at Walker's Point in Kennebunkport?" he asked me. "I'll have my people get with your people."

Well I don't have people, and my phone number is unlisted and restricted, but nevertheless, somehow, one day later my phone rang. I answered.

"Is this Brad Faxon?" a woman's voice asked.

"Yes, it is," I replied.

"Please hold for the president."

President Bush then jumped on the line and suggested a date for us to visit.

I said yes without even checking my calendar. I could have been scheduled to be at the US Open or British Open, but it wouldn't have mattered because this was the best invitation of our lives!

When the date came, we drove two and a half hours up from our house in Rhode Island to Kennebunkport. We pulled up in front of the president's home on Walker's Point, and there he was, President Bush, in typical khaki pants, a plaid shirt, leather belt, and topsiders. The former leader of the free world himself grabbed our luggage and brought it upstairs into the main house!

Phil Mickelson also came into Kennebunkport to visit on a number of occasions. During one of his visits, he and fellow PGA Tour star David Toms were at dinner discussing the unusual manner in which the Cape Arundel course records have been broken — and how Faxon had missed the putt and failed to break it.

"Maybe I will try to break the course record tomorrow," Mickelson suggested.

President Bush loved the idea. "That'd be great!" he exclaimed.

Mickelson, who has won almost every prestigious title imaginable and holds countless records, suddenly had the light of battle in his eyes. That night in the president's home on Walker's Point, as Mickelson laid his head down to sleep, he had his sights set on the course record at Cape Arundel Golf Club.

The next morning, I was at my desk at Cape Arundel when the president, Mickelson, and Toms arrived at the club. I was getting ready to head out to play golf with them when Mickelson ducked into my office and headed me off.

"Ken, before we play, please remind me," Mickelson asked, "are you one of the people who hold the course record?"

"I am not any longer," I told him.

"Well, I am thinking of breaking the record today, but don't want to do anything wrong here. How would the members feel about that? Would President Bush be okay with that? How do you feel about it? Will it be okay?"

I reconfirmed with him that I thought he should do it. "I am sure the president and our members would be excited and honored to have Phil Mickelson as their course record holder," I assured him.

"Okay then," he said, nodding. "I'll do it. I will go low."

Anticipation was high to see the course record broken by a Major Championship–winning, Hall of Fame golfer — one of the best of his era — when we got to the first tee. The opening hole is a 375-yard par-4, and so Mickelson could virtually drive the ball to the green. He teed the ball, took a swipe, and hit a booming drive . . . but his ball went down the left side of the hole. We had some long, gnarly fescue grass growing over there along the edge of the water. Mickelson's ball ended up right in that grass.

It took a while to find the ball, and when we did, it was in a spot where the grass was knee-high. Mickelson gave it a go with a swipe, but he "chunked" the ball and it only flew about four feet. So he was faced with a very similarly tangled lie in the same grassy area again. He hit the ball a little harder that time and "air mailed" the ball — it flew all the way over the green. There is a marsh behind the green surrounded by more thick sea grass, which Mickelson also then had to climb into to play his third shot — which he also chunked. Once he chopped it out just off the green we, out of courtesy, averted our eyes as Phil Mickelson, who'd only twenty minutes earlier asked for approval to break the course record, carded an 8 on the first hole and was four-over-par!

(He relaxed after that and still ended up shooting 63, which was one off tying the record — even after making an 8 on the opening hole. So, imagine what he could have shot!)

Toms, meanwhile, was quietly having a little party of his own.

While we were keeping an eye on Mickelson — and helping him find his ball — Toms started his round by making back-to-back birdies. From the tee of the 157-yard, par-3, third hole, Toms hit the ball with his tidy, measured swing.

He'd made birdie, birdie, and then an eagle by making a hole-in-one on the 157-yard third hole! Toms was four-under-par after three holes! (Remember the eighteen-hole record is seven-under.)

On the fourth hole, a 398-yard par-4, Toms was on the green in regulation — but he four-putted! The jinx was on! After all, Toms has won more than ten PGA Tour events, including the 2001 PGA Championship, but little Cape Arundel Golf Club bit him back. As Walter Travis himself said, "The game of golf starts on the greens."

Toms went on to shoot 63 that day.

Two years later, Mickelson and Justin Leonard came back to Kennebunkport and played a round at Cape Arundel with President Bush and Mark Plummer (who was one of the former record holders, having shot 62). During what became an interesting round, Mickelson found himself a few under par after the front nine, which to me is the easier of the two nines with more scoring opportunities.

Our "Amen Corner," if you will, at Cape Arundel are the twelfth, thirteenth, and fourteenth holes: The twelfth is a 409-yard par-4 that bends to the right along the cornfield; the thirteenth is a really great, 165-yard par-3 over water with swirling, prevailing winds that can be different at the green than they are at the tee; and the fourteenth, which is a 387-yard par-4, one of our longer holes, with a tough tee shot over water and woods lining the Kennebunk River down the left before you reach a difficult, little green.

Mickelson birdied each of those holes during the round and finished strong on the seventeenth and eighteenth holes to shoot 60!

Phil Mickelson had finally set the record he sought. A plaque with Mickelson's glove, ball, photo, and the signed scorecard hangs proudly in the Cape Arundel clubhouse.

Jerry Pate, US Open Golf Champion, TV Commentator, and Golf Course Architect

I played with "Daddy Bush" at Montgomery Country Club in Montgomery, Alabama. He was there, in his post-presidency, doing a speaking engagement for the Economic Development Partnership of Alabama.

We closed the golf course down. It was just us, a couple of local folks, and the Secret Service in front of us and behind us. We were running around the course. The president likes to play in under two hours. We were laughing and telling stories and I'd made some birdies and eagles. I wasn't even keeping score. On the sixteenth green, though, the president tapped his putt in and started walking toward our cart, but not before he told me, "Jerry, you're ten-under-par right now."

He'd been keeping my score on his card, too.

I was standing over an eight-foot putt for a birdie when he said this to me. I'd never shot 59 in my career, but suddenly I started thinking about the very real possibility of it happening on this day . . . with the former president of the United States in my cart to witness it!

So I was taking a little extra time to line up this eight-foot putt. While peering at the hole, I felt something over my shoulder and then heard a voice say, "Yep. Looks like right-edge."

It was President Bush. He was lining up the putt for me.

"Yes sir," I said. He felt the putt would break a little to the left. But I was thinking it was left-edge, which meant the putt would break a little to the right. "Let me just have a look at this and see."

I walked around to the other side of the hole and looked at the line from there. I became convinced. Hell yes, it's definitely a left-edge putt, I told myself.

So I walked back to the other side of the ball and just as I began to settle in over the ball the president said, "Yep. Knock it in. Right-edge."

"Ok," I said to humor him, but then President Bush spoke again.

"Knock this one in and birdie the last two and you'll break 60. Looks like right-edge," he said in that unmistakable voice of his. I remember thinking he really sounded just like the impression Dana Carvey had done of him on the show Saturday Night Live.

With all this in my head, I finally settled over the ball. I took my normal one practice stroke and looked down at the ball. Then I suddenly thought, Maybe it is right edge?

I decided, given the situation to split the difference. So I hit the putt on a straight line . . .

. . . and it broke out to the right and missed the hole.

So it definitely had been a left-edge putt.

Walking off the green I had the golf self-talk in my head: I am the dumbest son of a bitch in the world. What am I doing listening to the president of the United States read your putts? I wouldn't tell him how to deal with foreign policy in the Gulf War!

As it turned out I made pars on the sixteenth, seventeenth, and eighteenth holes and shot 62. I didn't shoot the 59 I thought I could shoot.

I was with President Bush on another occasion at a dinner in Palm Springs at the Eisenhower Center. It was a fundraiser celebrating the twentieth anniversary of the Betty Ford Clinic. It was a prestigious dinner because Betty Ford, Nancy Reagan, Rosalynn Carter, Barbara Bush, and Hillary Clinton were all there. The first ladies were the speakers and the men, including the two former presidents who were in attendance, Gerald Ford and George H. W. Bush, were just bystanders.

President Bush walked up to me and asked, "Whatcha been doing?"

I told him I'd been working on this and that and living in Florida.

"Give Jeb a call and play golf with him sometime," he said, speaking of his son, who'd just become governor of Florida.

"That's nice, Mr. President, but I don't know Jeb."

"Well he's your governor. Call him."

I laughed and said, "I'm not just going to call up the governor of the state and ask him to play golf!"

President Bush insisted.

So I called Governor Jeb Bush, and can you imagine that he invited me to Tallahassee, which was great since my son was attending Florida State University, and we played golf and had a lot of laughs. He was really nice to me, and I came to learn that's the Bush Family way. They're so cordial and open to sharing with friends. Jeb even eventually appointed me to a volunteer position on the State of Florida Water Management Board.

Davis Love III, a Major Championship winner and Ryder Cup Captain, also visited Kennebunkport, and President Bush invited me to play golf at Cape Arundel with them. Because we were playing with Love, a small gathering of members and locals were following us, watching Love and the president play.

Cape Arundel's sixth hole is the center-point of the property physically and visually. In a sense, it's the heartbeat of the course because the road into the clubhouse and parking area runs right next to the tee and green. People driving in and out get a chance to see a golf shot or offer a pleasant wave to whomever is playing that hole. It's a fun hole because it's a 116-yard, par-3 hole requiring a slightly downhill shot over a small pond to a sloping, terraced green.

The pin was in the back-right section of the green, and President Bush took a swipe that sent his ball online—seemingly destined for the hole.

"That's going to go in the hole," Love cried.

The ball hit the green, bounced twice, and was tracking for the hole. But it suddenly stopped and seemed to hang virtually suspended on the lip over the hole. We knew it didn't go in when the crowd moaned and sighed. How great would it have been for a golfing president to have a hole-in-one?! We looked at President Bush for his reaction.

Without missing a beat, he just joked, "I put too much feather on that one! Maybe I should have hit more club?"

His antics made it very funny because the ball was less than half an inch from going in the hole. Believe me, he did all he could do to get it there—it was so close to the hole there was nothing else he could have done.

Eric Higgins, 2007 Maine Amateur Champion

I had the special experience of growing up and shagging balls for Ken Raynor at Cape Arundel Golf Club — the same golf course our past president of the United States Mr. George Hebert Walker Bush plays. To have such a genuine, kind-hearted person like the president take the time to acknowledge me is very special. Since I once held the course record of 62 at Cape Arundel, President Bush used to greet me by saying: "Good morning '62 Man!'"

Through our love of the game I was able to experience lasting memories with one of most charismatic and genuine men I have ever met!

And I still can't believe that I played in foursomes with both the 41st and 43rd presidents and their PGA Tour friends including Phil Mickelson, David Toms, and Brad Faxon.

It wasn't just golf greats who came to Kennebunkport and Cape Arundel Golf Club. Athletes of every variety came to play with their friend the president.

Ivan Lendl, the great tennis player, initiated a golf career after winning every trophy imaginable with a racquet in his hand in the 1980s and early 1990s. The Czechoslovakian earned the nickname "Ivan the Terrible" mainly from competitors he coolly vanquished.

Lendl came to Kennebunkport often to play both tennis and golf with the president. Lendl was a good golfer who hit the ball hard. In tennis he was a power player who imparted a lot of topspin, so it made sense, but to be able to convert that power to golf and be proficient meant he was truly a great athlete. He really found passion in the game of golf. Lendl ended up playing some professional golf on mini-tours and won a celebrity tour event.

Rod Laver, World-Class Hall of Fame Tennis Champion

I played with George at Kennebunkport. I had a great time. It was an honor to be on his property. I was there with Jerry Weintraub, and it was a thrill to meet the president and Barbara, too. George showed me around his property. It was quite an exciting time.

We then went out and played tennis on the president's court. We had a great game and I was quite surprised that George was playing as well as he was at his age of eighty.

The president's arms reached far. You just never knew who would be coming to Kennebunkport. Some came only for lunch, but others stayed a while. Bar told me one season that they filled 750 beds with overnight guests at the invitation of the president during the summer months she and the president were there.

It was fun for the Cape Arundel staff to have such notable people coming and going. I always reminded them to answer the phone professionally, because they could never know who might be calling on the other end of that line.

Sometimes, it was the president.

"Kenny we're going to come over and play nine holes. Would you like to join us?" President Bush asked me.

"Sure thing, Mr. President. See you here," I answered.

Sometimes he'd tell me who he was bringing with him, sometimes not, and sometimes he'd tell me as an afterthought. On one occasion he mentioned he was bringing a guy with him, but I didn't recognize his name.

When the motorcade pulled up, President Bush and another fellow got out, and a beautiful woman emerged from the other side of the car.

"Kenny, you know Brooke Shields, don't you?" President Bush said.

I was totally unprepared for it. She must have just gotten out of the pool because her hair was soaking wet, which changed her appearance, and she had a white T-shirt on. Of course I remembered her from the movies *Blue Lagoon* and *Endless Love*, plus her famous Calvin Klein television commercials.

Her husband and the president were going out to play golf and they took me with them. Shields rode around with us for a while to watch.

The president also invited actress Teri Hatcher to Kennebunkport and brought her to play golf. Of course all the single guys in the club wanted to meet her and get an autograph with the woman who played Lois Lane on television in *The New Adventures of Superman* and was a "Bond girl" in the 007 movie *Tomorrow Never Dies*. When Hatcher left town, she had pints of frozen treats sent from Rococo, an artisan ice cream shop in Kennebunkport's Dock Square, to Walker's Point as a thank you gift.

President Bush obviously has a lot more flexibility during his post-presidency, where "relaxation" takes on a whole new meaning. As president, every moment on his schedule was spoken for, from the moment he woke up until he went to sleep. As former president, though, the world was his playground and he invited me into the playpen from time to time, including a "boys weekend" in Houston to visit with Roger Clemens, the superstar Major League Baseball player known as "The Rocket."

When Clemens pitched for the Red Sox, he used to make the eighty-mile trip up to Kennebunkport with Frank Viola, another Sox pitcher who was World Series MVP with the Minnesota Twins, and former second baseman Mike Andrews. Sometimes they'd bring other members of the Red Sox organization with them to play golf with the president. Ultimately, I got to know Clemens fairly well. He even asked me, on another occasion, to come down and represent the president at his charity golf tournament in Houston since the president could not be there.

The plan was to go play Lochinvar Golf Club, a private men's club just outside what is now known as George H. W. Bush International Airport. Lochinvar is a Jack Nicklaus–designed course that opened in 1980. Clemens was a member there, and celebrity golf coach Butch Harmon, who coached young Tiger Woods, was then the golf professional, having followed in the footsteps of his father Claude Harmon, who won the 1948 Masters Tournament and served as Lochinvar's pro for a spell.

I flew down to Houston and was welcomed as a guest to President Bush's home in Houston's West Oaks neighborhood near Tanglewood.

Dick Cheney was also in town, so he and his wife Lynne joined the president, Mrs. Bush, and me for dinner.

Going to a restaurant with a former president of the United States can be interesting. I have been fortunate to have dined out with POTUS on many occasions in many restaurants. The restaurant, having been notified, certainly expects him and has a table readily available. Depending on the location of the table and the type of restaurant, some people notice President Bush is there and some don't.

Usually throughout the dinner there is a noticeable amount of "hush," though sometimes people will approach the table and say something like, "Hello, Mr. President. I am sorry to interrupt your dinner but it's the chance of a lifetime. I just wanted to say 'thank you for your service.'" Or sometimes they just want to shake his hand and tell him he is their favorite president. Sometimes it is short and sweet; other times it is not.

"It takes just as long to say 'yes' as it does to say 'no,'" I have heard the president say many times. He understands that meeting a president is a cherished moment for somebody, somewhere.

Usually to make sure everyone is happy and feels included, and so the restaurant experience for the rest of the diners is not disrupted all evening, President Bush will say hello to people or nod and smile at them when he initially walks through and sits down.

It's fun for me to be a part of it. A lot of people think I am either Secret Service or one of his children.

The next day, we played golf at Lochinvar. The match was Clemens and me against Harmon and the president. Afterward, Clemens had a big barbe-cue at his house. Some of the other old Red Sox were there, including Rich Gedman, the catcher who was on the 1986 team that almost won the World Series (but infamously lost to the New York Mets in dramatic fashion).

Clemens's house was like an amusement park. In addition to the base-ball memorabilia and the in-home theater, Roger showed us his full-sized batting cage. Inside the cage was a Major League–sized pitcher's mound with a home plate and batters' boxes.

"Mr. President, would you like to grab a bat and step into the batter's box to see what a 100-mile-per-hour fastball coming over the plate looks like?" Rocket asked him.

I saw, for a flash, the light of battle in President Bush's eyes. It was clear that he loved the idea! After all, he loved baseball. As a left-handed first baseman who batted right-handed, he even competed in the 1947 College World Series, where his team, Yale, lost to California.

While at Yale, where his father had also played baseball, the man destined to be president met the great Babe Ruth. There is a very famous photo of the young Bush in his baseball uniform and Ruth in a suit and tie out on the diamond.

While in office, President Bush attended ten Major League Baseball games, throwing out the first pitch at eight of them, including the 1992 All-Star Game where he appeared with the most legendary Red Sox player of all time, Ted Williams. Six of the games he attended were in Baltimore, since Washington, DC did not have the Nationals yet. The president took Her Majesty Queen Elizabeth to two innings of an Orioles game, and the next April helped open the team's brand new home: Camden Yards. In 1991 President Bush threw out the first pitch at a Texas Rangers game in Arlington where his son, future president George W. Bush, owned the team. The Bushes often attend Houston Astros games, and even had front row seats for the 2005 World Series games. In 2016, at the age of ninety-one, President Bush, confined to a wheelchair, was all smiles when he threw out the first pitch (from close range).

So yeah, he wanted to try to hit a Roger Clemens fastball that day at his home in Houston.

Nevertheless, and perhaps much to the relief of the Secret Service, the president made a quip and declined.

Roger "The Rocket" Clemens, Major League Baseball Pitcher, Eleven-Time All-Star, and Two-Time World Series Winner
Growing up in Houston and playing professionally in New England I have had the fortune to cross paths many times with Mr. and Mrs. President Bush. Both of them have been super to me, my wife Debbie, and our four boys.

The golf game we had at Cape Arundel Golf Club with #41 and head pro Ken Raynor was a good one! I believe we set a new "ground-speed" record: eighteen holes in just under three hours, no practice swings needed!

Then it was off to Walker's Point for a nice lunch (Barbara did it up for us all) and for what I thought was to be a casual toss of horseshoes.

Boy, was I wrong. It was competitive!

After a brief warmup, President Bush and I were on the same team. He leaned in and said to me, "Look, bear down! I don't want to lose to those boys down on the other end! Game on!"

That single moment is the reason I have a horseshoe pit in my backyard in Houston.

The day after we played golf and went to the barbecue, we took a plane and flew over to Austin to meet up with President Bush's son George W. Bush, who was governor of Texas and would, of course, become the 43rd president of the United States. We planned to go play golf at Barton Creek Country Club with

Hall of Fame PGA Tour player Ben Crenshaw, a two-time Masters Tournament winner who'd raked in twenty-nine total Tour titles.

Crenshaw is a longtime friend of the Bush Family, especially #43. They're both Texans and have known each other for a long time. Ben has come to Kennebunkport a number of times and appeared on behalf of Barbara Bush's literacy foundation. As a golf course architect and a lover of traditional, golden-age golf, Crenshaw loved playing, and inspecting, our Walter Travis–designed, century-old, Cape Arundel golf course and its green complexes during past visits to Kennebunkport.

It was pouring rain during the first portion of the round at Barton Creek, but you would never know it was raining at all from the way the former president just focused on his game and the friendship. Luckily the weather cleared out and we were able to finish the round. We laughed along the way as we hit shots and made some putts. When you're on the golf course, you have four guys that have no titles to their names. They just have a fun time playing as four golfers — not as a president or a Masters winner or a governor/future president, or even a golf pro. It was just four guys who loved the game of golf and enjoyed the camaraderie.

Governor Bush had to leave fairly quickly afterward because he had some business to attend to before hosting a Christmas party at the Governor's Mansion, which he invited his father and me to attend. President Bush and I had some time to kill before the party, so we went out with one of the Barton Creek assistant golf professionals and played another eighteen holes — this time on the course Crenshaw designed.

After all that golf there was still more! On the way to the Governor's Mansion for the Christmas reception, the Secret Service agents took us to the headquarters of Golfsmith, the giant golf retailer founded in Austin in the late 1960s, which grew to have over a hundred retail stores nationwide before eventually struggling and being bought by Dick's Sporting Goods. Golfsmith, at that time, was interested in doing a custom club-fitting for the president. They were pleased to have a golfing president and felt it was good for the game. Many in the golf industry were also very pleased with the way President Bush had a reputation for playing quickly. Reporters described the president's speedy style as "aerobic golf" or "cart polo." But in truth the game of golf suffers from slow play, because it clogs up golf courses with people standing around waiting to hit their shots. Golf is somewhat time-consuming as it is, but it ultimately is a sport, so players should keep it moving. Not everyone can play as quickly as President Bush, but they can try, at least, to keep up with the group in front of them.

The staff at Golfsmith HQ shop was thrilled to have the president in the store hitting shots on the club-fitting monitor. The club-fitters were examining his swing and noting the result of his shots into a net. The data and observations helped them determine what degree of loft his driver should be and a suitable length and flexibility for the shaft.

President Bush enjoyed the session so much we were late for the governor's Christmas party. So as not to cause a disruption, we were brought in the back door of the mansion and ushered up the back stairs so we could each get a quick shower and change out of our golf clothes and into proper attire.

The Texas Governor's Mansion, built in 1856 and since expanded and renovated, is in the middle of a block in downtown Austin. It's historic and stately, with large white columns and trees and gardens all around it. It's elegant yet warm, with a grand, U-shaped staircase curving up to the second floor. There is a large parlor, with yellow walls and white decorative molding, used for entertaining. The mansion's library is used for less formal entertaining and contains the desk of Stephen F. Austin — the father of Texas — along with his portrait. There is a neat tradition on display, in that there is a collection of personal items from past Texas governors, including Ann Richards. Richards, when she gave the keynote speech at the 1988 Democratic National Convention, made fun of the occasional gaffes of Republican Vice President Bush, who was running for president, by saying: "Poor George he can't help it; he was born with a silver foot in his mouth."

Obviously Bush went on to win in spite of Richards, and his son George W. Bush got an extra measure of revenge by beating Richards and becoming governor in 2004.

Post-cleanup, we went downstairs to Governor Bush's party as quickly as we could. Governor Bush delivered a very moving prayer to the attendees about the troops away from their families and how much it meant to him to have his father with him at the Christmas gathering.

Ben Crenshaw, Major Championship Winner and Accomplished Golf Course Architect

Having known the Bush Family for so long, this picture, taken at the Governor's Mansion in Austin, Texas, typifies the generosity and kindness of the man we have loved for so long. President Bush had just finished a golf round with me and his son, George W., who was governor at the time, and of course went on to become president.

Our girls came over to visit, and the president, without hesitation, was interested to read a report that my daughter, Katherine, had written about him!

Katherine is on the left in the picture, and Claire, clutching her doll, is on the right. It's a lovely memory of his loving spirit.

Despite the celebrity status that many of them held, perhaps the best part of these interactions, for me, was that sometimes friends of the president became friends of mine—like Jerry and Jane Weintraub. Jerry, who passed away in 2015, lived countless different show business careers in one life, with success as an actor, talent agent, and award-winning producer. He made John Denver a star and organized the first-ever stadium tours for the likes of Frank Sinatra, Elvis, Neil Diamond, and Led Zeppelin. Weintraub also produced films that are still popular today: *Nashville*; *Karate Kid*; the three *Ocean's* films, in which he had cameo roles; *The Firm*; and more, including Disney's live-action *Jungle Book*.

Weintraub, who had a home on Blueberry Hill near Cape Arundel Golf Club in Kennebunkport, also produced a documentary about President Bush for HBO titled *41*, which had its premiere at a big party on the grounds of St. Ann's Church in Kennebunkport and at Walker's Point celebrating the president's eighty-eighth birthday.

I found myself in California to do some work with the Titleist golf company. With a couple of extra days on my hands, I went to Los Angeles to see Weintraub. I got to his beautiful Malibu home late one evening. After breakfast the next morning, Jerry took me over to Sherwood Country Club where we played golf with the PGA professional there and one of Jerry's friends.

Sherwood's golf course was designed by Jack Nicklaus, and it is a Hollywood hangout. The mountains, visible from the course, boast the peaks seen in the opening credits of the long-running television show *M*A*S*H*, and they used to shoot car chase scenes for the show *Dukes of Hazzard* in the valley's rugged scrub. Once the course was built, it hosted high-profile golf events such as Greg Norman's "Shark Shootout" and Tiger Woods's "World Challenge." Hardcore golf fans will remember the primetime, made for television, live "Showdown at Sherwood" in which David Duval, in 1999, squared off against Woods under floodlights to create "Monday Night Golf." (Woods edged Duval.) The Champions Tour has held tournaments at Sherwood, too.

As we played golf that day, we were one of only two foursomes on the golf course for the entire day! We spotted another group playing the front nine while we were playing the back nine. Once we got close enough, I realized that none other than Wayne Gretzky was in the foursome.

Since we were playing opposite nines, both foursomes finished at the clubhouse simultaneously. So we ended up all sitting down at one table and having drinks after our respective rounds. Gretzky seemed to enjoy going up and getting hors d'oeuvres and bringing them to us at the table. Imagine, the player dubbed "The Great One" playing waiter at a very exclusive Hollywood golf club. And there I was—all due to President Bush.

Tim Finchem, PGA Tour Commissioner

The first time I met President Bush was in 1989. I had Sam Snead on a three-day book tour because in our new publication, which was a history of the PGA Tour, Sam Snead had been named as the number-one player, historically, which was a somewhat controversial pick.

Sam and I went into the Oval Office to meet the president.

"Sam, I'd love to get a lesson from you," he promptly told Snead.

As can only happen in the White House, a staffer came forward with a manila envelope full of golf balls and a wedge. We then all went behind the White House onto the lawn and got right to it hitting some golf balls.

As the president did that, Snead leaned over to me and said, "The president needs a little work."

His propensity for hitting balls on the White House lawn was an indication of just how much President Bush loves the game.

I've met "The Great One" and "The King" — all thanks to President Bush.

When people get an invitation from the president, they usually respond in a positive way, even if they are a "King"! Arnold Palmer came up during the presidency, in August of 1991, to Kennebunkport to visit President Bush and to play golf at Cape Arundel.

"The King" arrived in Kennebunkport mid-afternoon, and we went out about 4:00 p.m. to play some golf.

"I love this golf course," Palmer exclaimed. "It reminds me a lot of Latrobe."

Latrobe Country Club, outside Pittsburgh, was Palmer's home course in the summer and, like Cape Arundel, a nice, little, simple place to play. (He played out of Bay Hill Club and Resort, on a course he designed, in Orlando, in the winter months.) Palmer's father Deacon, who became the superintendent, helped build the original Latrobe course in 1920, and he and his son Arnold modernized it with the creation of the eighteen-hole course now there. Like Cape Arundel's river, a creek runs through the Latrobe course, and Palmer added covered bridges to represent the charm of Pennsylvania's past. Palmer owned the course and his ashes, after his passing in 2016, were spread on the course. By the time of his passing, Palmer had played golf with presidents Dwight Eisenhower, Richard Nixon, Gerald Ford, Ronald Reagan, both Bushes, Bill Clinton, and Barack Obama.

President Bush and I played with Palmer and Dick LeBlonde, who was a dear, longtime friend of the Bush Family. It was great to get out there and break the ice with Palmer. We'd planned to play eighteen the next day, so that late nine holes gave me the chance to meet him and get rid of the butterflies.

The next day we had a gallery of a hundred people or so waiting to follow us around as we got ready to play eighteen holes on our little golf course. Word gets out when a high-profile visitor comes to play golf, and so we have to be a little careful we don't end up with thousands of people out there. Parking was an issue and big crowds meant more work for the Secret Service, but we, at the club, became used to it. But the opportunity to get a glimpse of Palmer was an invaluable experience for our members, and the president, not blind to the fact it was good for the members and for Cape Arundel's reputation, was comfortable with it. There are no gates to enter or gallery ropes or anything to contain the members, so when they came to watch as spectators they could stand right next to the tee with Palmer on it and even approach him. People were excited but polite; they gave Palmer space, and he returned the gentility by being engaging and friendly and signing autographs.

One of our employees at Cape Arundel was Rob Souza, a hard-working, high school senior who loved the game of golf. So I decided to give him the opportunity to caddie for Arnold Palmer. Souza got dressed in his "Sunday best" golf attire to come caddie for Palmer. When he was introduced to Palmer, a big moment for the kid, Palmer took one look at his navy blue sweater and winced.

"What happened to the Palmer attire you should have worn today?" Palmer asked.

Confused, Souza looked down at his sweater, which was embroidered over the chest with a little "Golden Bear" — the logo of Jack Nicklaus! Palmer, historically, was a rival with Nicklaus on and off the golf course. Their businesses competed for golf course design projects, apparel, and even wine. Of course, Arnie was having fun with him, but Souza was red-faced. He was horrified he hadn't even thought of it.

Souza, as I mentioned, was conscientious and enterprising, so he put Palmer's golf bag down, took his Nicklaus sweater off, turned it inside out, and put it back on. He caddied the entire round with the sweater inside out to conceal the Golden Bear logo.

Our maintenance staff was more aware of Palmer's endorsements and sponsorships. The club had an old Massey Ferguson tractor from the 1950s with the big pontoon tires on it. Our superintendent, knowing Palmer was coming, parked the tractor in a very visible spot by the seventh green and put a quart of Pennzoil on the hood of the tractor! Palmer saw the Pennzoil on the tractor when we passed by it and loved it.

He also got a big kick out of listening to the president's trademark golf acclamations: "Take a bite out of that one!" "I put a little feather on that one!" "Mr. Smooth strikes again!"

I've been honored to play with President Bush over hundreds of rounds, but I'd never played with Palmer. He hit the ball a lot lower than the players today do. He was a powerful man who hit bullet line drives instead of launching the ball high.

We all wanted to play well and hit some good shots, and I, as the host PGA professional, really had a responsibility to do that. We reached the fourth hole and I was at even-par, but I really did not hit the ball on the clubface or hit anything solid. I was getting the ball out there, but not in a professional manner. So off the fourth tee I scraped another drive down the middle. It wasn't hit very well. As I was walking from the tee toward the fairway, I felt an arm come around me. It was Palmer's arm.

"Ken," he said, "I know you're a little frustrated about your game but you're doing fine. You're swinging just a little fast."

I looked Arnie in the eye, as President Bush walked by, and said, "Well I am a little nervous playing with Arnold Palmer."

Palmer got a kick out of that knowing the president of the United States just walked by, but I was more nervous about playing with him!

My mother and father came out to see Palmer, too, and I got to introduce them, along with my father-in-law Chuck Forrest, who was a champion club golfer himself, to Arnie after the round. No one in my family played golf, but the importance and celebrity of Palmer transcended golf, and everyone was thrilled to have a photo with him on the porch of the clubhouse.

Arnold Palmer may have been known as "The King," but actual royalty, the Duke of York, His Royal Highness Prince Andrew, came to Cape Arundel Golf Club for a round with President Bush on September 22, 1999.

HRH Andrew is the third child of Her Majesty Queen Elizabeth and her husband Prince Phillip, the Duke of Edinburgh. At the time of his visit, he was fourth in line to the throne behind his older brother Charles, the Prince of Wales, and Charles's two sons William and Harry. After a career in the Royal Navy, he served, in 2003, as captain of the Royal and Ancient Golf Club of Saint Andrews, the world's ruling body of golf outside America.

The duke was able to visit Kennebunkport because he was in the area attending the Ryder Cup matches at The Country Club in Brookline, Massachusetts, about one hundred miles to the south.

It was quite an interesting scene when the duke arrived in his Royal English Limousine with old-fashioned fenders. He was friendly, but at the same time I'd discussed with my staff some of the protocol about being in the presence of royalty. For instance, we were to address him as "Your Highness," and certainly not as "Andrew."

I was in the foursome with the duke, President Bush, and Dick Thigpen. I remember that Prince Andrew was a fine golfer. He made two birdies on the front nine and his 35 certainly made a statement.

Following the round we requested that he might sign the club register, which he was fine with doing, but, as royalty, he did not sign autographs.

That round at Cape Arundel may have been the highlight of Prince Andrew's week, since the United States beat the Europeans in dramatic fashion at the Ryder Cup in Brookline.

HRH Prince Andrew, Duke of York

I have the greatest good fortune to have George Bush Sr. as a friend, and whilst we have enjoyed each other's company on many occasions in different circumstances around the world since he left office as the 41st president, my fondest memory is playing or watching golf with the president.

I knew from reputation he was a player of some repute with little time for slow play. Well, I have experienced his lack of slow play on more than one occasion, but the first was the most memorable playing in Kennebunkport with him in September of 1999.

I am not the slowest player in the world and I know that we should do all we can to reduce slow play, but nothing prepared me for the speed and accuracy of playing golf at the George Bush rate! It was a marathon pace and we never let up; it was exhilarating. The fascinating thing was that our scores were no worse for playing at such speed; in fact I might suggest that playing at a higher tempo actually allowed me a better score.

The course is his local so he knows it well and, of course, is at an advantage over any unsuspecting opponent! I wasn't that unsuspecting and I found it the most enjoyable game because we chatted about the world and played the game as we chatted at a speed that meant we went round in just around two hours and thirty minutes. I can only do that on my own at Swinley Forest Golf Club at home, but I've never been able to achieve that on any other course.

It is a constant golfing memory that I am truly grateful for having the opportunity to experience and a lesson to me that I have used on numerous occasions to encourage others to play golf in a similar manner, to reduce the scourge of slow play afflicting our great game.

We were excited about having the Ryder Cup matches nearby at The Country Club, in Brookline, near Boston. Brookline is a special place for me—my dear friend Mark Whitney, one of my true golfing buddies I played college golf with, is a member there. In my much younger days he and I played hooky many times from school in Maine to drive down there and play golf in the springtime since the weather there was better. The Country Club was built in 1893 and designed by Scotsman Willie Campbell. It was the course upon which twenty-year-old caddie and amateur golfer Francis Ouimet upset British golf legend Harry Vardon to win the 1913 US Open after an eighteen-hole playoff, a story which was featured in the 2005 film *The Greatest Game Ever Played.* (Shia LaBeouf played Ouimet.)

I happened to be an officer in the New England PGA in 1999, and Ed Carbone was the executive director of our PGA section. PGA professionals from New England, especially officers, were needed to help with the facilitation of the Ryder Cup. Carbone phoned me before the matches.

"Ken, I am going to give you one job during the Ryder Cup," he said, "and that job is to get President Bush to make a visit to our New England PGA hospitality tent during the Ryder Cup."

I thought to myself, *How am I going to direct the president to go into that tent?* I never wanted to overstep my bounds when it came to President Bush. After all, he was my friend first. It was hard, sometimes, not to cross that line, as I understood why people were asking me to intervene and get something from the president for them or their charity or whatever their need might be. I always tried to use my discretion in deciding what was right or what was wrong and what I should or shouldn't do.

During the Ryder Cup matches, my wife Anne and I were roaming the course and watching some of the shots. We ended up sitting with the president and assorted members of his family, including his nephew Hap Ellis and his wife Robin, who were members of The Country Club at Brookline, in the grass along the sixth hole. We were watching the long-hitting players trying to drive the green from a tee shot up on the hill.

"I'd like to walk over to the twelfth hole," President Bush said.

Luckily, the New England PGA tent was in between the sixth and twelfth holes, so my opening had fallen right into my lap!

"Sir, I've been given a very large responsibility," I confided. "Would you mind stopping into the New England PGA tent on the way?"

As gracious as he was, of course he agreed to do it. They asked him to sign the registry book and our executive director, plus many New England professionals, got to meet the former president.

After the tent visit, we made our way over to the twelfth hole, and while we were sitting on the hill, one of the Secret Service aides came over to the president.

"Excuse me, sir. Michael Jordan is in the crowd and he'd like to come say hello."

At this, the former first lady popped right up. "George, he's my friend! I'll go get him."

Bar went down into the crowd and escorted the NBA superstar over to visit.

Jordan was very cordial. The first thing he did was greet the children there, including my son Kyle and a number of the Bush grandchildren. Those were the first hands he shook as he made his way toward the president. I remember eventually shaking his very large hand and it made my hand feel like a little baby's hand!

Jordan sat with the president and Bar, chatting and watching golf.

When Jordan left, he went to all the little kids again and gave each of them a high-five.

I feel fortunate that Cape Arundel has provided me a venue at which I have been able to witness how the president can unwind with friends and family.

When I stand on the porch of the clubhouse, overlooking the Kennebunk River, I can clearly remember occasions on which President Bush would come up, while he was in office, without enough time to play golf, but time enough to sit on the porch or hit a few putts on the practice green below. If the weather were bad, instead of playing golf, he'd spend fifteen minutes standing there on the putting green in the driving rain with a fishing pole I'd stored in my office casting into the river to try to catch an elusive striper, which he did many times.

The Bush Family has had a big impact in putting Cape Arundel in the limelight. In order for us to show our appreciation for that, our board of directors, led by Pierce O'Neill, along with former president Gary Koch, was involved in a special idea—to name the clubhouse in honor of President Bush, our nation's 41st president. We, therefore, named the clubhouse "41 House." We have a nice plaque on the clubhouse signifying the club's love for President Bush and his love for the golf course.

The 41st president was very humble in his reaction to naming the clubhouse after him. As always, he presented a genuine "why me" attitude.

6

ANCHOR TO WINDWARD
WALKER'S POINT, KENNEBUNKPORT

Walker's Point is an incredibly beautiful, eleven-acre piece of property jutting out into the Atlantic Ocean with a cove on the west side where the boats can be moored or docked. Tourists can view the home and the compound, take pictures from an observation area on Ocean Avenue, and enjoy an incredible sight of Maine's Atlantic coast and the sea.

In addition to the twenty-six-room, wood-shingled main house and the other homes used by the Secret Service agents and the Bush children and family members, the property has tennis courts, a horseshoe pit, swimming pool, a putting green, a small shed with fishing equipment, a giant flagpole, and even a windmill, which President Bush jokes that he put up to please former vice president Al Gore, a strong environmentalist.

The home next to the main house is called "The Wave." It's more of a cottage. It's a stand-alone building. The most recent addition to the compound is a home Governor Jeb Bush built.

When you drive in off Ocean Avenue, if you are approved and make it past the security gate, you pull up and the office is on the right. Even just going into the office there to drop something off or pick something up, it's going to be memorable. Their office is a revolving location of lots of different activities from all corners of the world. Whether he's signing autographs or sending letters, it's a busy office.

I used to go down every once in a while to get something autographed, like a book or a photo, for different people who'd asked me to do it for a charity or a favor. It might be someone the president knows asking for the autograph, or maybe they happened to meet him at the club and subsequently brought in a printed photo taken during their encounter. I would follow through to finish the task. As the president believed, "It's just as easy to say 'yes' as it is to say 'no.'" He loves people and their stories.

The interior of the house is decorated in a "beachy," summer cottage fashion, with warm cushions and incredible vistas of the ocean on three sides. The sea is the focal point, but there's a great fireplace in the living room that creates a warm, cozy Maine feeling. The president has a chair he sits in, which every guest quickly understands. Mrs. Bush does, too, and she almost always has a jigsaw puzzle going in the corner. There are pictures all around the house of their family, including multiple pictures of special family outings and memories.

Larry Gatlin, Country Music Star, 2017

Dear Mr. President,

I wish that you or any of your sons or George P. were the president of the United States right now.

On second thought, I kinda wish Mrs. B were the president of the United States right now. She would REALLY kick some rear end.

I love you all.

Keep the Faith,

Larry

Walker's Point, a peninsula jutting out into the Atlantic Ocean, is home to the American competitive spirit: tennis, putting, and horseshoes. The president himself is very competitive.

There is a horseshoe pit on a strip of land between the house and the ocean, and family, friends, and world champion throwers have witnessed many games there. The president, as a Walker's Point Rule, instilled the "six pack," which means the top ringer gets all the points. Why? Well, for one reason: It speeds up play.

One story makes me chuckle when I think of playing horseshoes with the president. On one particular occasion, as part of the Gary Pike/Mercy Hospital golf fundraiser (which became known as the George H. W. Bush Celebrity Golf Classic), the Titleist head of club-fitting I worked with, Jim Lumadue, had come to Cape Arundel Golf Club to present the president, who was playing the event, with a set of custom-fitted Titleist golf clubs.

Jim came up the day before the event and I had the chance to take him over to Cape Arundel for a quiet, friendly round of golf with President Bush and Jim Nantz. On the eighteenth tee, the President asked me, "You're coming over for dinner tonight, right?"

"Yes," I answered. "Bar invited us over. We will be there."

Then he turned to Leumadue and asked, "Jim, you play horseshoes, don't you? We'll have a game before dinner, because you're coming to dinner with Ken, right?"

Jim responded, "Yes sir, I will be there. I'm looking forward to it."

We played the eighteenth hole, and when Nantz and President Bush got into the SUV and were driven away, our guest quickly turned to me with a panicked look on his face.

"Ken, we've got to hurry up and get back to your house before we go to dinner. You have to teach me how to play horseshoes!"

He'd never played before in his life.

When we got back to my house I briefed Jim about what to expect when we got to Walker's Point, and we threw a few horseshoes for practice as well.

When we eventually got to Walker's Point, Jim did the best he could to fake success at horseshoes. After all, some of the great world champion horseshoe players have competed at Walker's Point, so it's as if you're playing on sacred ground. They throw a ringer almost every time, which the president loved watching. Himself a left-hander who uses the "flip-toss" technique, he cites his ringer percentage at 30 percent.

During Walker's Point horseshoes games, the pressure can be high. Sometimes members of the Bush Family will come and sit on the stone wall that runs along the horseshoe pit and separates the promontory from the

ocean. If they do that, they're more than just spectators, though, they participate: with cheers, jeers, catcalling, heckling, and roasting of the competitors.
Cheers for a ringer. Boos for a bad one. Newcomers can be startled by the
merciless, vociferous nature of the running commentary.

Mrs. Bush, for instance, might call out to someone playing poorly by
saying, "I'd try to give you some encouragement, except you're not showing
me any potential!"

Patty Rhule, a writer for *USA Today*, came up to the Point to write a La-
bor Day article about horseshoe tossing.

"My mother taught me to lose with class," the president told Rhule. "'Be
a good sport, George. Don't ever throw your racket again. Stop crying and
go out and practice!'"

Practice is one way to improve your ranking. But the Bush Family also
has a fictional, but often discussed, governing body for all competitions,
whether the game is horseshoes, golf, or tennis, dubbed "the Ranking Committee."

"We'll bring it up in front of the Ranking Committee," you might hear
Doro or Bar or the president himself say when determining the skill of a
competitor. Sometimes the mythical Ranking Committee is invoked to determine who partners with whom in doubles tennis. If someone hits a good
shot, one of them might yell out, "Call the Ranking Committee," as if to
notify them of an improved performance.

As a joke, someone once framed a photo titled the "Ranking Committee," which now hangs on the wall inside the Bushes' home. It's a photo of
#41 looking very presidential in his jacket and tie and lapel pin, and with
him are a Native American chief, a motorcycle gang member, a lady from
India wearing a turban, and a construction worker. On close inspection of
the photo, though, each of the faces of the people are actually faces of President Bush, superimposed!

When you say "bring it up in front of the Ranking Committee," you can
bet it's all President Bush making the decision as to whether you make the
cut on the golf course, tennis court, or oceanfront horseshoe pit!

Tim Finchem, PGA Tour Commissioner

President Bush is such a lovable man. From time to time he would ask me to stay in Kennebunkport to visit him and spend the night at his Walker's Point home. On one occasion, as we were turning in for the night, I told him, "I won't see you in the morning because I have to leave early to travel to a commitment."

"Why don't you at least have a cup of coffee with us? What time are you leaving?" President Bush asked.

"6:00 a.m.," I told him.

"That's fine," he insisted. "Come down early and we'll have a cup of coffee."

So I got up extra early in the morning, got dressed, and went down into the kitchen, where I came across a member of the house staff.

"The president said you might have a cup of coffee with him?" he asked.

"That's right," I answered.

"Well here is the cup of coffee," he said, handing it to me. "Take it and go on into the bedroom."

With some hesitation, I walked into the bedroom of George and Barbara Bush. They were sitting up in bed watching the morning news.

"C'mon and sit down, Tim," said President Bush, gesturing to a chair.

As usual, they made me feel right at home.

The Bushes' home on Walker's Point has suffered storm damage during the time the president has owned the oceanfront home, which he bought in 1980 after spending virtually every summer of his life growing up there.

On one occasion in which stormy weather foiled the president's outdoor plans, Boston Red Sox pitchers Roger Clemens, Frank Viola, and second baseman Matt Young were invited by him to come to Kennebunkport to play golf. The president was looking forward to it and so was my golf staff. After all, the great "Rocket" would be right on our golf course!

The forecast, though, took a turn for the worse. Meteorologists, in fact, were predicting a hurricane might hit the Maine coast. We were watching the weather closely because it is not often a hurricane hits New England. Having originated in the Bahamas, Tropical Storm Bob turned into Hurricane Bob when it reached the evacuated Outer Banks of North Carolina on August 18, 1991. That meant sustained winds of one hundred miles per hour and gusts even higher were tracking toward Maine.

At 4:30 that morning, my phone rang. It was the president.

"Kenny, what do you think? Are we going to be able to play golf today?"

"Okay, Mr. President. I'll be heading over to the golf course shortly. We've had some rain. I will take a look at the conditions."

Now, only moments earlier, on the television news, I'd seen that Mikhail Gorbachev, the Soviet leader, was missing. A coup had been staged against him. And with Moscow hours ahead of us, the events unfolding surely had provoked the early awakening of the president, who naturally would be concerned about who had control of the Soviet Union's nuclear weapons. And yet his ability to compartmentalize his attentions still had him wondering whether the golf game with Roger Clemens was on . . . in the moments before a hurricane strike! (It turned out Gorbachev was under house arrest in his vacation dacha in the Crimea and the coup only lasted two days.)

What ended up happening that day, though there would be no golf, is that Clemens and company would at least come for breakfast at Walker's Point. It was a nice breakfast made more interesting in that President Bush was in and out, spending at least half the time on the phone dealing with the Soviet crisis and consulting with Gen. Brent Scowcroft, his national security advisor.

After breakfast, President Bush, Clemens, Viola, Young, and I stood on the back patio of the house looking over the ocean and watching the sea seem to grow more and more turbulent right before our eyes. The Walker's Point grounds crew, for safety, was putting up sheets of plywood over all the windows on the ocean side of the house.

Hurricane Bob made landfall the next day in Rockland, Maine. Portland, near Kennebunkport, received over eight inches of rain.

But that was nothing compared to what would come two months later, a nor'easter that became known as "the Perfect Storm." The tragic sinking of the Atlantic fishing boat, the *Andrea Gail*, which was written about and

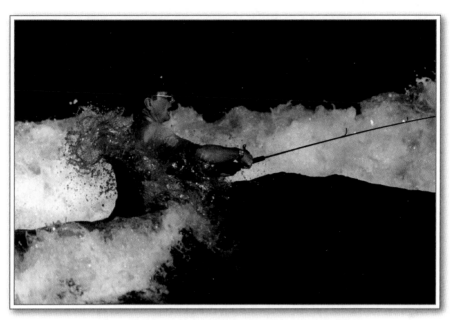

When it comes to "man vs. fish," President Bush is competitive and courageous even in the surging surf. (*Photo courtesy of Bass Pro Shops*)

President Bush, proud of his "bucket list" tarpon catch, signed and sent this photo of himself and George Wood to Bass Pro Shops founder and fishing friend Johnny Morris. (*Photo courtesy of Bass Pro Shops*)

Just "one of the guys"—who happened to have been president—enjoying a day on the Gander River in pursuit of Atlantic Salmon. *(Photo by Ken Raynor)*

Golf professional and president doing what they both enjoy—fishing in the Kennebunk River in a boat built by Booth Chick, a Kennebunkport legend. *(Photo by Anne Raynor)*

A presidential scrum to address the world media after a round of golf at Cape Arundel Golf Club in Kennebunkport. *(White House photo)*

General Brent Scowcroft, Vice President Quayle, and I observe President Bush trying out what was one of the very first swing trainer apparatuses. (*White House photo/Susan Biddle*)

Besides broccoli, President Bush despises bugs, but they never stopped him from either fishing a river or playing golf. (*White House photo/Susan Biddle*)

Birdies or bogeys, you'd always get a Bush smile. (*Photo by Barbara Bush*)

The Raynor family cozy on a cart with the president and his "future caddy": our son Kyle. (*White House photo*)

While the gathered media anticipated he'd take their customary questions, #41 playfully put the cart in reverse and we sped backward onto the course. (*White House photo/Susan Biddle*)

Friends—President Bush and Ken Raynor—completing a round of golf (better known as "cart polo") in under two hours. (*White House photo/David Valdez*)

Jubilation with CBS Sports anchor Jim Nantz and me after the president played his last regulation shot, on his 86th birthday, on Cape Arundel's par-three 6th hole. The photo was taken by the president's daughter Doro Bush Koch.

King, President, and Pro: Arnold Palmer, George H. W. Bush, and Ken Raynor. (*Photo by Frank Symosek*)

The self-described "Mr. Smooth" with his pro enjoying his favorite "home" course, Cape Arundel, which reminds him of times with his family and friends. (*Photo by Barbara Bush*)

The president clowning around, showing the "kid in him," while lining up a putt for the crowd and cameras. (*White House photo*)

President Bush's last drive as Commander in Chief was off Cape Arundel's 18th tee simultaneously with the First Lady and myself. (*White House photo/David Valdez*)

The old Naval Aviator enjoying the co-pilot's seat of the DC-3 heading north to the Arctic to catch Char. (*Photo by Ken Raynor*)

A proud moment welcoming the president and Mrs. Bush as Cape Arundel celebrates my twenty-five years of service and that of superintendent Greg Searles. *(Photo by Chris Smith)*

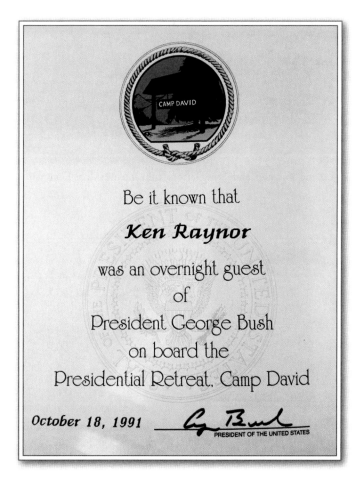

GEORGE BUSH

May 2, 1995

Dear Ken,

Here's another item for our Cancer auction. I played yesterday
with Butch Harmon and Davis Love. I think I played the very
worst golf of my entire erratic golf life. I had some new irons- Pro
Gear. They did not suit me, so back to the Cobras I go. The Pro
Gear woods seem fine. I now use the new Titanium S Yard
driver. I like it. One problem- the ball goes straight too much. I
allow for my slice, and wham, the straight tee shot comes off the
Titanium like a rocket and I am in the deep stuff on the left.

I will be open for business on Walkers Point May 11th. Don
should get to Kport May 4 at the latest. Ariel and Paula leave here
May 4 with Millie in Bar's car.

See you soon. All best,

GB

P.S> Oh yes, Davis Love outdrove me on every hole!

One of many, many amusing, endearing letters from the president I cherish.

10-11-00

Ken + Ann -
Thanks for all you do to
give great happiness to all
the Bush family Love to all
3 of you - G Bush

From his Kennebunkport home to mine—a
touching card we treasure.

President, Prince, Pro and Pal: an incred-
ible round with President Bush, HRH
Andrew—the Duke of York, myself, and
Dick Thigpen at Cape Arundel.

Roger "The Rocket" Clemens got to Kennebunkport just before the hurricane did while the Bushes were boarding up. (*White House photo*)

turned into a movie, occurred during this monster storm, which ultimately caused hundreds of millions of dollars in damage and further loss of life beyond the New England fishermen aboard the boat.

On October 30, 1991, while the president was in Washington, the Atlantic waves of a nor'easter were so high they crashed up over the roof of his two-story home at Walker's Point. Ocean Avenue, the only road leading to Walker's Point, was closed because it was completely submerged by the tides.

The thirty-foot storm surge crashed right through the home, causing the Bushes to lose everything on the main, lower floor. A lot of the big, heavy deck planking was lifted up by the waves and the boards ended up being driven through the home like battering rams. The powerful, unstoppable ocean waves took a couch they never saw again and an entire piano disappeared in the storm. The Secret Service agents, after the storm, found four-hundred-pound boulders in the middle of the house. The carpet, all pushed up against the wall, had been replaced by pounds of sand, mud, seaweed, and dead lobsters. The massive dining room table was in the yard and one wall of the Bushes' bedroom was missing.

The storm caused major damage to the house and the loss of some irreplaceable family memorabilia.

The president and Mrs. Bush were finally able to return to the partially restored home months later on Good Friday, April 18, which was, ironically, a snowy day.

Sometimes, when we had golf scheduled but the weather was bad, President Bush, who'd allocated the time and had been looking forward to the golf, would come down from Walker's Point to the club anyway and visit or autograph things that had been sent to him there or dropped off. We'd sit at my desk, I'd put the photos or books in front of him, and he'd sign in what seemed to be rapid-fire fashion. He never minded adding a name or a personal note with the autograph, and we'd talk about life and goings-on while he signed.

The president was a fan of ensuring that people often left Kennebunkport with autographed, and sometimes personalized, memorabilia. On one occasion, the annual trustees meeting of the PGA Tour's "First Tee" program was meeting in Kennebunkport.

The First Tee program is a cooperative designed to make golf, and the life lessons it teaches, accessible to young people who otherwise might not have an opportunity to try it in rural and urban areas. Through in-school and after-school programs at practice facilities and participating golf courses, the First Tee teaches, in addition to golf, values like integrity, respect, and perseverance.

President Bush was the honorary chairman, so we wanted to make it special for the captains of industry and golf industry leaders who attended and came to play golf at Cape Arundel, including PGA Tour commissioner Tim Finchem and Joe Louis Barrow, the son of the great boxer Joe Louis, who was the executive director of First Tee. Those trustees left with personalized, autographed gifts from the president.

One year, Cape Arundel Golf Club member Gary Koch, a Minnesotan, created an inter-club match against Hazeltine Golf Club, in Chaska, Minnesota, where he is also a member. The golfers from Hazeltine, which has hosted Major Championships and a Ryder Cup match, came to Kennebunkport to face off against a team of golfers from Cape Arundel Golf Club in the Prescott Cup, named for George H. W. Bush's father and brother, with the spirit and intensity of a Major Championship. We developed a beautiful tournament logo, had it enlarged with gold leaf, and President Bush signed one for every competitor. He personalized each one, such as *"To Gary, Cape Arundel's Best! George Bush."*

As the host and head professional, one of my responsibilities was to organize these gifts and get them signed and framed in time to have them presented at the tournament dinner that night. It came right down to the wire in receiving them, which meant at 4:00 p.m. that day I was still down at Walker's Point while the president was signing and writing personal messages on them. There were at least twelve guys on each team, which means there were at least twenty-four items to be signed . . . and the clock was ticking.

I had a list of names, which I was checking to make sure each one was spelled correctly as the president signed and personalized them. And guess who was helping out, handing each large print to the president to sign? House guest Brian Mulroney, the former prime minister of Canada! He was a Walker's Point houseguest at the time and offered to help. So here I am, a hard-working golf pro, and I've got the former president of the United States signing commemorative prints and being assisted in the process by the former prime minister of Canada. Who says you can't find good help anymore?

Mulroney had come to Kennebunkport a few times to visit President Bush. Mulroney, who was prime minister for nine years, through 1993, was a very good singer and liked to sing Irish songs in particular. Many of us heard his talents firsthand during a sing-along in President Bush's living room. Grammy Award–winning Christian singer/songwriter Michael W. Smith, who was also there, played the piano for us, and sang some of his hits, including one of the president's favorite songs called "Friends."

Roger Whittaker, who has sold millions of albums worldwide during a long career, also came to visit once, post-presidency. He was born in Kenya to English parents, and now lives in Ireland, after releasing hits such as "Durham Town," "New World in the Morning," and "The Last Farewell."

The nurses who traveled with and looked after President Bush during his time in the White House, knowing his taste in music, teasingly bestowed upon him the title of "President of the Roger Whittaker Fan Club." Five or six years after his presidency, he invited his nurses, whom he hadn't seen since he was in office, to come to his home in Kennebunkport for a "Reunion of the Roger Whittaker Fan Club." They all loved his music, but none had ever met Mr. Whittaker. So when the nurses came to see the president and have a fun weekend, President Bush surprised them with the presence of the actual Roger Whittaker, whom he'd secretly invited!

President Bush had also invited Anne and me, so after a wonderful dinner at Walker's Point with the nurses we all went into the living room and sat on the couches or on the floor just like it was Christmas morning. It was very casual, with or without shoes, and Roger Whittaker sang songs, played requests, and helped lead a sing-along.

The nurses also had a surprise for President Bush. They had a presentation for him. They'd put together a "Presidential First Aid Kit." It was a tackle box, and in each of the drawers, they'd put a first-aid item with a written memory attached to it. For instance, one drawer had Band-Aids and the note: "When Mr. Bush got a blister." One of the nurses would then get up and tell the story of how, when they were in Moscow, the president needed a bandage. Another drawer had a pill in it. By the time they were done, it had become a comical rehashing of all the medical assistance they'd provided for him through their tenure.

It's clear to me, based on the interactions I've witnessed at Walker's Point and other places, that the president and Mrs. Bush have such warmth that people feel parental affection from them. Jim Nantz thinks of the president as a second father. In fact, when Jimmy decided to propose to Courtney, now his wife, he brought her to Walker's Point.

Nantz, who is the anchor for CBS Sports's golf coverage, proposed to Courtney, who is very successful in sports management, in a very suitable manner—he took her to the practice putting green beside the Bushes' home.

In the hole, he'd placed the engagement ring, so that when Courtney sunk a putt, she'd reach down to retrieve her ball and also find the ring.

Someone in the Bush Family videotaped the putting display and the joyous emotion when she eventually did sink the putt and find the ring.

Jim Nantz, Emmy Award–Winning CBS Sports PGA Tour, NFL, and NCAA Anchor

I remember occasions where we'd be out with the president on his boat , "Fidelity," on a sun-splashed afternoon along the Maine coast. It was between lunch and dinner and we'd been out on the seas enjoying a little getaway with the president at the controls, followed by a Secret Service flanker boat with agents. President Bush would pull the boat right into Ogunquit or any of those idyllic, little New England harbor towns — so many of them are just alike. On multiple occasions, he wanted to go pick up an ice cream cone. He knows, in all these seaside towns, where to stop and where the ice cream shops and restaurants are. He also knows where the "Barnacle Billy's" of the world are where he can get his lobster roll.

On one particular occasion, he pulled into the dock and we stepped into what is basically the center of town to have an ice cream. We walked up to the ice cream window and he took his place standing in the back of the line. I could see the startled looks on the other people's faces.

"Oh, Mr. President, step right up here," a lady said. The others in the line agreed with her and began parting the way for him.

Well, President George H. W. Bush is never cutting a line. He's never going to do that.

"Here, please," the people said. They were literally begging him to let them do something nice for him.

"Thank you, but you were here first," he said with a smile.

He's just not comfortable with cutting a line. He will wait. He's a gentleman.

Often the Bushes' warmth extends beyond those they consider lifelong friends. I recall one time, post-presidency, when #41 and an intimate group of people were bunkered in for dinner at the Cape Arundel Inn, which, from Ocean Avenue, overlooks the Bushes' home on Walker's Point in Kennebunkport. I noticed a middle-aged woman, obviously a tourist, who'd seen our table but seemed very nervous approaching. Nevertheless, she finally got up the courage to come over and, politely, introduced herself to the president.

"Well nice to meet you. How are you?" he asked her.

"I just wanted you to know how much I admire you and we miss you being in office," she said, nearly breathless.

"Thank you very much. Where are you from, dear?"

"My daughters and I are visiting from Pennsylvania," she answered, and then, with the ice broken and her nerves subsiding due to his welcoming, reassuring nature, the woman began rapidly telling the president a lot of details about where she was from, what she did, and why she admired him.

President Bush gestured to his right. "I'd like to introduce you to my wife Barbara."

"Barbara Bush!" she cried, "Oh! I'm so sorry, Mrs. Bush, I didn't see you sitting right there. It's so rude of me! Of course, what an honor to meet you, too . . ."

And then the woman began telling Mrs. Bush, who was smiling and nodding, that she was visiting from Pennsylvania and the details of her trip, until President Bush gently interrupted her again.

"How about I now introduce you here to Brian Mulroney and his wife Mila. He was prime minister of Canada for almost a decade."

"Oh, wow, prime minister! Of course," the woman said, once again embarrassed because she'd been so rattled and focused on President and Mrs. Bush she virtually hadn't acknowledged anyone else was even at the table.

Then President Bush said, "Here, while you're here, this is the great singer and actress Jane Weintraub! You've maybe known her as Jane Morgan on Broadway." (Morgan, who has a star on the Hollywood Walk of Fame, summered in Kennebunkport and sang for five US presidents.)

The Bushes enjoy situations like this and opportunities to meet fellow Americans and make them comfortable. The woman, thrilled by the whole experience, returned to her family with a story to tell.

A short time later her Pennsylvania family finished their dinner and could not walk by President Bush without another stop.

"Mr. President, can I just interrupt you one more time, as I'd love my daughters to meet you," she said.

With a big, warm smile President Bush was pleased to have a chance to say his favorite word: "yes." He stood and welcomed two beautiful, fashionable young women who reminded him of his own granddaughters. He began asking all about them and what schools they attended.

"Are you enjoying Kennebunkport and Maine? What are you doing to-morrow?" he surprised them by asking.

"Oh, well, it's Sunday, so we're planning to go to church in the morn-ing," the woman answered.

"Oh yeah? Where?"

"We'd planned on St. Ann's."

"That's my church. What time?" the president asked.

"Eight o'clock."

"No kidding? That's when we go. We'll probably see you there," he said. "After church, would you all like to come over to the house and take a dip in my swimming pool?"

Mrs. Bush turned and looked at me and said, "I just knew he was go-ing to do that!"

"How did you know?" I asked her.

"Because George does that all the time!"

I can't help but chuckle when I recall this memory. After all, Walker's Point is all about interactions with the people, and if that wasn't the quintes-sential example of such interactions, I'm not sure what is!

7

FISHING, *FIDELITY*, AND FUN

When he heads to Maine in the summer and gets on that stinkpot of his — a 36-foot cigarette boat named Fidelity — *the good ol' Texas boy comes out in him. Our president becomes a yahoo through and through.*

—Tony Chamberlin, in his "Woods and Water" column in the *Portland Press Herald*

I stood on the front porch at my home in Kennebunkport flipping through the mail. A puffy letter in the pile was embossed with a simple return address: "The White House, Washington."

I opened the envelope to find some fishing lures and a letter dated August 6, 1989 with the signature on the bottom: "George."

The letter was from President Bush, and it read:

Dear Ken,

I'm sitting here on Sunday evening thinking about trying for the blues, the stray mackerel, or even the river striper.

Here are a few lures that might bring you some luck.

Hang in there. See you soon. I, plus four rods, plus my long putter, will be there in 10 days (or so).

All best,

George

Imagine being surrounded by the majesty of the White House and under the pressures of the Oval Office and, as the leader of the free world, still allowing yourself a few minutes to think about the daydreaming about the pleasures of fishing? Not to mention taking the time to write your friend and express that sentiment? He did that for many of us.

That's George Bush.

On another occasion, in 1990, I received a large envelope in the mail—again with the White House return address. I carefully opened it and tugged out what was an official-looking document with a blue border around it and the gold "Seal of the President of the United States" on the top. A banner title below the seal read "National Fishing Week, 1990."

It was a presidential proclamation extolling the importance of recreational fishing in America, how important it is to the economy, and saluting how the pursuit is a peaceful and rewarding way to spend time alone or in the company of family and friends. It concluded: *"NOW, THEREFORE, I, GEORGE BUSH, President of the United States, by virtue of the authority vested in me by the Constitution and the laws of the United States, do hereby proclaim the week of June 4 through June 10, 1990, as National Fishing Week . . ."*

The president's signature, of course, was on the bottom. I thought this proclamation, and the fact that he'd mailed it to me, was really neat. And then I noticed the president's handwriting on the bottom of the proclamation: *"Ken—When I signed this I thought of you. —George Bush."*

Was I humbled?

Honored?

Proud?

Flattered?

Oh, all of those and about seven thousand other emotions! Most of all, I was hoping we'd have time together soon.

Our love of fishing comes from our love of the outdoors. Mother Nature, in her grandeur and beauty, is where it all starts. Breathing good, fresh air, feeling alive, and waking up in the woods is special. As a young boy growing up in South Salem, New York, I was able to roam thousands of acres of forest in my area. I spent many days of my youth in the tops of trees, in tree forts, while camping. I'd start in the backyard and then end up way out in the woods. I was very involved in Scouts. I was very lucky, from the age of eight through seventeen, to be able to attend Forest Lake Camp for Boys on 825 acres up in Warrensburg, New York, near Lake George because my Uncle Phil and Aunt Mae Confer owned it. A lot of my growing years for a month or two each summer were spent at that camp. I enjoyed being down on their 1.5-mile stretch of lakefront fishing for perch and bass. They offered field trips to go mountain climbing on the Adirondacks, and I was always the first one to sign up. As I got older the field trips lasted three or four nights climbing the high peaks of the Adirondacks, such as Mount Marcy and Algonquin, both of which are over five thousand feet high. I did that multiple times and fished the Adirondack Lakes for little brook trout and pike, which increased my knowledge and instilled my interest in the outdoors and fishing.

My dad also took me to the wilderness of Northern Maine's Baxter State Park to go fishing. He and I would paddle out into big Harrington Lake in a canoe, set up a tent on an island, and spend a week up there fishing and bonding. We still laugh about some of the adventures we had out there. It really exposed me to the outdoors.

Picking a college in Maine had a lot to do with my love of the outdoors. And, of course, living in Kennebunkport, Maine, in a state where we have fresh rivers and the mountains meet the sea, we have the benefit of being able to fish for both freshwater and saltwater species. Cape Arundel Golf Club is right on the Kennebunk River, and the fishing there is very good. We've caught striped bass and even a Coho salmon in that river. We have sea-run brook trout, with two tides a day — you can set your clock by them — as the river rises and falls eight to ten feet.

My love of fishing has only continued to grow and to get to share it with the president and so many other experts has been very fulfilling. The president's love for being on the water is apparent, and we both enjoy watching the sun rise or set with a fishing rod in hand.

Fishing is a science. The old saying is that 10 percent of the fishermen catch 90 percent of the fish. That's because good fishermen understand where they are fishing. They understand technique. They're throwing flies into ambush areas, not just into the water hoping the fish find it. Good fishermen go into specific areas with specific tides and areas relative to the tides. They know the moon phases. They know the temperature of the water, whether it be tropical water or fresh, running, oxygenated water. For instance, if you have low, warm water for a long time it's much more difficult to catch Atlantic salmon anywhere. Has an influx of rain chilled the water down? Will the salmon, therefore, be more active? There's definitely a science to fishing. The president started to really learn more about that in his post-presidency, by fishing more often with experienced friends. He has even said he likes cleaning mackerel to see what they've been eating because it helps him to know when the bigger fish are coming in.

President Bush would tell you that his fishing career started in Kennebunkport when he was a little boy trolling for tinker mackerel off the back of his grandfather's thirty-three-foot lobster-style boat and that now, all these years later, he loves taking his grandkids out fishing on his own boat. He's also admitted to meditating while he fishes. He's got as many fish on the wall in his office in Kennebunkport as he does anything else marking his accomplishments, which tells me he really loves fishing and cherishes the memories of his fishing adventures.

President Bush started by using fly rods off the rocks of Walker's Point next to his house. We used fly rods targeting Atlantic salmon and sea-run trout up in Labrador and, in the Northern Territories, we had the opportunity to hook a world-record Atlantic char with every cast.

The president has become a passionate fly fisherman. He has learned how to drift the fly, strip the line, and double haul when he's casting to extend the length of his cast, as all experienced fly casters know the importance of reading the flow of the river and controlling the depth of your fly. He's had help from great guides in the rivers and from his friend Billy Busch, a consummate fisherman who loves fishing for stripers in Kennebunkport. Most days when the president went fishing, Busch was in the boat. He was very dedicated to the president.

Further south, Boca Grande, Florida, is renowned for its tarpon fishing because of the Boca Grande Pass, but it's also well-known for Charlotte Harbor—270 square miles of shallow water that provides many species of fish, predominately snook, redfish, sea trout, and cobia. Many times, when the president visited Boca Grande at Christmastime, we'd go out into Charlotte Harbor in pursuit of these species of fish. We had friends and guides who went with us, including Phil O'Bannon. Phil would take us out, leaving bright and early in the morning, and returning about four o'clock in the afternoon.

We'd do some sight fishing—that is, trying to see the fish even before casting. So we'd have a spotter on a bonefish skiff up on the platform trying to see them. The skill then is trying to cast right into the fish's window so the fish takes the strike because you cast the fly into their feed lane. If you land that fly right in front of them, it's like you've put a wonderful-looking piece of steak right in front of them and they don't want to leave it alone, so they swim over and grab your fly.

"That one's in his house!" President Bush would yell if he made an accurate cast, hoping to get a strike in return. You could just sense the joy he received. But part of the joy is having the right fly, the right color, and the right depth to get a strike from a fish you've seen before you even cast.

Everybody always wanted President Bush to catch a big fish, and he knew we'd try to put him in the best spot to do that, but I think he was even more excited when one of us caught a big one.

Our time out there, often, was focused and quiet because of the type of fishing we were doing. Sometimes we'd talk about the cast, the "almost," and the one that got away. The fishing talk is kind of like a golfer who recounts his round and tells how it could have been his best ever if only that putt hadn't lipped out. Every fisherman has "almost" caught that trophy fish after a ten-minute or longer battle.

At the end of the day, we'd salute the "fish gods," but it was always about a day with Mother Nature and friends.

Our interaction at sea in Kennebunkport would often take place while he was on his boat *Fidelity* and I was on my twenty-three-foot Seacraft boat, *FinAddict*, and we would rendezvous out there and fish. We always shared fish stories, or information about where to find the fish or what type of new "secret" lures we were using to catch them. Sometimes, if we crossed paths I'd have to joke, "Sorry, Mr. President. The blues were just jumping all over the water just down past Parson's Beach."

There were plenty of times our boats would pass each other in the river as we were going out for a quick ride or coming in from a cruise. It was always fun for people I had aboard my boat because, here we were going out for a little sunset cruise at six o'clock at night after a busy day at work, and we'd encounter the *Fidelity* in the river. The next thing they know my guests are saying hello to the commander-in-chief and whomever he might have in his boat—anyone from Jim Nantz to Phil Mickelson to Mikhail Gorbachev. The president was always good about waving to those aboard my boat and stopping to talk for a bit. Then we'd hear the roar of his engines as he raced to get back to Walker's Point in time for dinner.

President Bush and I did enjoy fishing the Kennebunk River, which ran by the Cape Arundel Golf Club, many times. Sometimes we would fish off the riverbank below the putting green trying to catch the elusive striper. Even in the rain, since he's an active man, President Bush would come to the club and stand casting into the river while a shower fell overhead. Rain or shine, it did not matter. To him it was about making the most of the time he had at a place he loved.

Near the end of his term in the White House, President Bush was in Kennebunkport and he phoned to ask me if I could "do him a favor" and stop by his house. Of course I drove over to Walker's Point as requested. When I got out of my truck, President Bush, who was outside waiting for me, introduced me to a friend of his in the driveway.

"Kenny, meet Johnny Morris. He's the owner of Bass Pro Shops."

Being a fisherman, I was very aware of what Bass Pro Shops meant for the sport of fishing and the fishing gear industry. Morris, a fishing enthusiast, founded the company in 1972 and grew it to more than one hundred stores and Tracker Marine Centers across the country. His Outdoor World stores are like museums and amusement parks with aquariums, bowling alleys, huge wildlife mounts, and restaurants. One hundred twenty million people visit his stores every year, and on top of that, in 2016 Morris would make a $4.5 billion deal to buy Cabela's, a chain of similar, competing stores.

He introduced a boat, motor, and trailer package called "Tracker," which has been the best-selling fishing boat now for nearly forty years.

One of these aluminum Tracker boats was sitting on a trailer in the driveway. I looked at the boat and did a double take when I noticed the writing on the side. It read "Son of FinAddict."

"It's for you, Ken. I want you to have it. It's a gift," the president said.

I was speechless.

"It's just a way for me and the Bush Family to thank you for all the help you've given at the golf course every summer and all the fun we've had," he said.

Still, I was shocked by the gift. His friendship was great enough thanks for me. I did what I did for him and the Bush Family out of love for them and love for my professional calling. There was no gift necessary. To get a boat like this was totally unexpected and over the top. Meeting Johnny Morris was a gift, too, as we have become lifelong friends.

> **Johnny Morris, CEO of Bass Pro Shops**
> *Sometimes President Bush drove the Secret Service nuts! The agents accept a certain amount of risk-taking in their position, but the president's level of risk-taking in his pursuit of fish was off the charts. He'd have cleats on his waders at Walker's Point and go climbing along these slippery, slimy moss-covered rocks along the shore to cast for striped bass . . . and the agents would have to follow him! It may have been the most risky thing they'd ever done.*
>
> *He is one of the grandest gentlemen I have ever had the pleasure to be around. He is a true American hero.*

President Bush thought it was fun to fish the Kennebunk River near the golf course in the boat because it had a nice, little trolling motor. And that is exactly what we did together many times in the years after his presidency. And it wasn't just about fishing. It was about watching a sunrise over a misty river with South Church behind us. Kennebunk River in that little boat at dawn offered a perfect atmosphere to relax. Or as one reporter who observed us but was bothered by the mosquitoes reported: "a lot of swatting, not a lot of catching."

"Swatting" was part of the sport. One thing that irritates all fishermen, and irritated President Bush as much as anybody, was . . . bugs. Mosquitoes, deer flies, gnats, sand fleas, you name it. If there were bugs around, he'd sense them. Though he'd be the first one out there in the rain with a rod ready to go fishing, bugs he could have done without.

Up in Labrador and Newfoundland, there were thousands of pests during some of the years. There were times we'd take garlic pills for days before
the trip because bugs don't like garlic and therefore would not bite as readily. One of the areas we fished in Labrador was called the "Sand Hill" and the
flies there were unbearable. They were so thick in the air that we could not
breathe deeply or we would inhale thirty or forty bugs. When we looked at
our hands they appeared solid black because they were covered with flies.
Sometimes the mosquitoes were so bad we'd see fifteen of them on one of
our hands when we tried to reel a line. We always powered through it using
fly dope or mesh mosquito hats as protection in pursuit of trophy fish.

Sometimes meeting and just "talking fishing" was all he had time for,
but that was just fine. He has an old fishing shed on Walker's Point that used
to be a small gardener's shed. It's probably only ten feet by eighteen feet. It
has eighty-year-old lumber on it and is all weathered from the sea. It is one
of the president's joys. It offers some serenity, and provided a great diver-
sion from the pressure of the office while he was president.

Different fishermen had visited him in it, including the great Ray Scott,
the founder of Bass Anglers Sportsman Society, who'd left some flies or
tackle.

"Here Kenny, take these. I'm sure you'll catch some stripers with them,"
he'd say, handing me some flies, which are artificial flies tied to various-
sized hooks with feathers meant to simulate baitfish on the water.

"No, no, Mr. President. You don't have to do that. I don't want to take
your flies," I responded.

"Well, then, do me a favor. Take them with you and try them another
time. Keep me posted on how they work, and we'll use them together next
trip.

Sometimes we'd open up a fly box and go one by one looking at each of
the flies in the box, using our imagination about what kind of fish we might
catch with each fly. We'd go to the shed, re-spool some lines, and just have
some interaction together with a fishing rod in our hands. On occasion, I'd
tie some flies or repair rods and reels for him, since his enthusiastic grandchildren, as anyone can understand, could be tough on the fishing equipment. I'd offer to take them home and fix them, but he'd insist we work on

them together, shoulder to shoulder. That's because the picture was bigger than just repairing reels. It was about shared time and friendship.

When President Bush would be back in the White House, I'd get hand-written notes from him wondering how the blues were running that week. "The blues" are a bluefish—an aggressive fish. They're incredible eaters with great choppers and teeth on them, so you don't want to get your fingers in their way. When you find them in the ocean, they're aggressive, so you're going to get bites. A striped bass may not always hit, but a blue will.

Tides were more important than time of day when it came to finding blues. Sometimes they were right on shore. They might be right on Kennebunk Beach near the jetty. Sometimes the president would go thirteen miles out to Boone Island, where he might see some whales on the way and enjoy the boat ride. He likes to drive full-throttle with the Secret Service fast astern as you might expect of a naval fighter pilot.

In Maine, because it is cold water, the blues are a solid, muscular fish. They run between sixteen and eighteen pounds so it's a great fight, and you can catch many of them if you are lucky enough to find the school.

The president, while he was in office, didn't really have a lot of time to fish for hours and hours, so if he found blues he was sure to come home with some fish—or at least some fish stories. The blues were that kind of fish. He enjoys a variety of styles of fishing, but he loves the burst of energy he gets from the quick strike of the blues.

Striper fishing was more about presentation in the surf. They'll follow the herring bait or glass minnows, or sand eels, and you can find them on the beaches, in the surf, or in the estuaries and rivers up the coast from Virginia north to Maine. The Chesapeake Bay is a spawning ground for stripers. So is the Hudson Bay area in New York. The New Jersey shore, Nantucket, and Cape Cod all offer wonderful striped bass fishing. Maine is about the end of the line for stripers. They don't go much farther north than probably Bar Harbor. So in Kennebunkport we're right in the middle of some very good striper fishing.

Andy Mill, who competed in two Olympic Games (1976 and 1980) as a downhill ski racer, came to visit often and is a good friend of President Bush. After being married to a Miss California, he was married to tennis star Chris Evert for eighteen years and, after his skiing career, became a champion tarpon fisherman, having authored the world-renowned book *A Passion for Tarpon.*

Mill also loved golf, so on his first visit, President Bush brought him to play Cape Arundel. I joined them, and literally four minutes after coming off the eighteenth green we were down by the river and I had a striper on the line of my fly rod. Mill could not believe he had been playing golf only moments earlier!

Andy Mill, Olympic Ski Racer, Champion Tournament Fisherman, and TV Host

It was always extraordinary going fishing with President Bush. The transportation was certainly overwhelming, with private jets and champagne and stone crab, but being in his presence was the most overwhelming part about it.

He loves fishing as much as anybody. Nobody fished longer and harder than he did. He always wanted one more cast and one more fish. He is such a good pal and a man's man. Even when we had a gazillion mosquitoes swirling around our heads, it never dampened his enthusiasm for fishing and being outdoors. He always wanted to talk about fishing and playing good golf. I think his passion for competition and sports was even evident during his presidency, since he relied on golf, tennis, fishing, running, and even horseshoes to relieve the immense pressures of that job.

I hosted a television show called Sportsman Journal, *but I never even dared to bother the president by requesting he be a guest on my show. One day, though, during his post-presidency, he approached me and asked, "Andy, why haven't you ever asked me to be on your show?!"*

I laughed and told him I'd love to have him on. Then, with an almost child-like look in his eyes, he asked me another question:

"Andy, do you think you could help an old man catch a big ol' tarpon?"

I could tell it was one of his "bucket list fish," and I really hoped I could help him. Talk about pressure! I got a hold of a friend of mine, George Wood, who is a guide in the Florida Keys, and President Bush flew down to go fishing. I never prayed so hard in my life to the "fish gods" to have him catch a big ol' fish!

We got just the right tide while we were chumming this channel and had President Bush throwing the fly. In the meantime we were putting some baits

> *out there in hopes of catching one on a spinning rod. Sure enough, he hooked a "fatty!" We chased that fish down and he was fighting it and fighting it and was already eighty-two years old at the time!*
>
> *"Please," I prayed, "let him catch this fish!"*
>
> *When we finally caught this fish, and resuscitated it and brought it into the boat, and put it in the president's lap and took a photograph, he was so elated that he literally had tears of joy in his eyes with that big ol' tarpon.*

The carrier *Yorktown* was steaming along the coast of Maine past Kennebunkport, so the ship stopped to invite and allow then-Vice President Bush and his guests to come aboard and pay a visit to the crew and officers. The *Yorktown* anchored a mile or so off Walker's Point. A launch came in to take many family members and invited guests out to the ship, but the vice president, of course, took his own boat, *Fidelity*, first circling the ship in true Bush fashion!

Sailors escorted each guest onboard, and the crewmembers, all lined up and dressed in their whites, greeted us, which was impressive and humbling.

Once aboard, guests, including the Veep and Mrs. Bush, were given a tour of the ship, which included the engine room for those interested. There was also an opportunity to meet the captain and enjoy a bite of food.

Standing on the bridge of a ship like that was overwhelming. Everyone invited cherished the event as a monumental experience, but the sailors, too, seemed to enjoy the opportunity to meet America's vice president. Bush's enthusiasm, though, seemed tenfold, given that he had served in the US Navy himself and had the opportunity to spend some time with those young cadets serving their country.

One summer, another famed vessel, the majestic US Coast Guard tall ship, the *Eagle*, sailed to Kennebunkport. The ship, mainly used for training for cadets and officer candidates, makes a limited number of port visits each year. It was not only exciting but beautiful to see one of America's great tall ships here in Maine.

Can you imagine being a cadet sailing the high seas and having the opportunity to welcome aboard the president of the United States? It was the Fourth of July 1989, and, in true fashion, the president and Bar invited many close friends to board the Eagle off the coast and watch the town fireworks.

Here I was, standing with the president and yet another special guest, George Zambelli, the most successful fireworks manufacturer/producer in the world, viewing the pyrotechnic show his company was performing. Zambelli explained to us how the fireworks worked and why they exploded in the patterns and shapes and colors they did.

PGA Tour star Phil Mickelson is another guest who spent time on the Kennebunk River with the president. On one particular occasion, they motored up the river and came across a large but quiet gathering of people on one side of the riverbank. A wedding reception was just getting started.

"Let's crash this wedding," the president said to Mickelson.

"Mr. President, we can't do that," Mickelson protested.

"Now, now, watch and see how this goes," President Bush reassured him.

He pulled the boat over and they got out and walked up the dock and into the gathering. Right in the middle of the reception, everything stopped as the attendees and bridal party instantly recognized him

"Hey, I didn't get my invitation!" joked President Bush. And, gesturing, he said, "Neither did my friend Phil Mickelson here!"

People broke out their cameras and they started taking pictures with the president, the bride and groom, and various family members.

When they were walking back to the boat, President Bush looked at Mickelson and said, "I told you that would be a lot of fun!"

Meanwhile those left at the wedding reception were asking themselves, "What just happened?!"

Stephen and Alicia Spenlinhauer are great friends of the Bushes, live up the coast from Walker's Point, and have a beautiful boat in Kennebunkport. They are an integral part of an Independence Day tradition that developed in town. The president's chief of staff, Jean Becker, hosted a fun barbecue every year at her home. I enjoyed being the "grill master" for Becker, cooking up the hamburger and hot dogs in the American, Fourth of July tradition. Lots of members of the Bush Family, along with many locals, staff (past and present), and an extended network of friends, became the traditional guests on the invite list.

After the barbecue, some of us would go down to the harbor and board the Spenlinhauer's eighty-five-foot Hatteras yacht named *Fine Print*. Spenlinhauer, or his captain, would idle us up the Kennebunk River toward the ocean to the cheers of the crowds waving from the shores.

One of his former captains was Bob Danzilo, who now captains *The Rugosa*, a classic New England wooden lobster boat, for ninety-minute tours of the Kennebunk River and the Atlantic coastline, including Bush's Walker's Point home.

He was captaining charter boats in Ft. Lauderdale when Spenlinhauer, who summers in Maine, coaxed him to come north. On Danzilo's first night in Kennebunkport, Stephen told him he wanted to take some friends on a fireworks cruise so he hired him to captain his yacht—a fairly standard request.

"I started to welcome guests aboard," Danzilo remembers, "when I noticed President George H. W. Bush and Mrs. Bush, plus other members of the Bush Family, and other very famous, powerful people getting on board. It was quite a surprise."

No matter who was captaining, many years we'd find a nice spot just outside the river where we would float around and watch the evening's fireworks.

The elder President Bush loves giving rides aboard *Fidelity*. His son, then President George W. Bush, in June 2007, brought Russian president Vladimir Putin to Kennebunkport, and they went fishing, but it was the eighty-three-year-old former president powering the boat over the Atlantic waves at top speed, which, according to #43, at first startled the macho Putin. They were all in it together at that point, and Putin, by the way, was not the only world leader to show some trepidation about boarding *Fidelity*.

But boating has a way of bringing people together—whether it's between communism and democracy; Democrats and Republicans; or current rivals and former rivals. Republican former president George H. W. Bush eventually flew around the globe with Democratic former president Bill Clinton—the man who denied him a second term by beating him in his bid for re-election, and was eager to welcome him aboard *Fidelity*, too.

Tim Finchem, Former PGA Tour Commissioner

In 1999, then sitting president Bill Clinton was the honorary chairman of the President's Cup Matches, which were held in Virginia outside Washington, DC. President Clinton was there at the time when former president Bush came to see some golf and support the event. I took Bush out onto the golf course in a cart. At some point while we were out there, a Secret Service agent came and whispered in his ear.

Bush then turned to me and said, "Tim, I've got to go now."

"Why?" I asked. "We're just getting started. Is everything okay?"

He answered, "The Secret Service just informed me that President Clinton is arriving on the property. We don't both need to be here at the same time."

With that he was gone. In his true deferential form, he did not want to distract from the presence of the sitting president in any way.

Greg Norman, PGA Tour Major Championship Winner and International Entrepreneur

When President Clinton was holding the office and made his first visit to Australia, I received a phone call from the White House saying that he would like to play golf with me while Down Under. Not being a Democrat, and hesitant to accept the invitation, I decided to reach out to my friend, President George H. W. Bush, to seek his advice on how to handle the situation. My conversation went like this:

"President Bush, I have had a call from the White House. President Clinton is coming to Australia and they want me to play golf with him. I am not a fan and I don't want to do it."

"Greg," the president answered, "my advice to you is to respect the position of the president of the United States — no matter who it is. I highly suggest you play golf with him."

"Yes sir."

I did end up playing a round of golf with President Clinton and I also ended up striking up a wonderful friendship with him. The lesson I learned from President George H. W. Bush that I still carry with me to this day, is to never pre-judge anyone.

During the Christmas season of 2004, both George H. W. Bush and George Bush spent time with former president Clinton, when the three joined hands to support a fundraising initiative for those suffering from the destruction of the tsunami in Asia and Africa, and subsequently to aid in Hurricane Katrina relief as well. As a result of their work and their new friendship, former president Bush (#41) invited former President Clinton (#42) to come stay with him in June at his seaside home on Walker's Point in Kennebunkport for a few days of golf and fishing and quiet relaxing out of the public eye.

Jim Nantz, Emmy Award–Winning CBS Sports PGA Tour, NFL, and NCAA Anchor

In March of 2005 I was working for CBS at the NCAA Final Four basketball tournament in St. Louis. I was in the cavernous, domed arena at a practice the day before the national semifinal game. Roy Williams, the coach of the favored North Carolina Tar Heels, was having a private conversation with me. I happened to have my phone in my hand while we talked and the ringer buzzed. I peeked down to see the readout of the caller ID: "Bush 41."

I went into a small moment of panic. I wondered what I should do. I was having private access to the coach (who by the way went on to win the semifinal and then his first National Championship a few days later on Monday night) . . . but it was the former president calling.

"I'm sorry, Roy," I said as politely as I could. "I can't help but see I have an incoming call from President Bush. I hate to bail out of this conversation. I hope you understand?"

Williams was great about it.

I went to a place backstage where I could hear the call.

"Jim, I've got a favor to ask you," the president said.

When he said he "had a favor to ask," I knew he was not about to ask for a favor, because he doesn't do that. He doesn't ask for tickets. He doesn't ask for access. He's not going to do anything ever to put you out. Usually, when President Bush tells you he's "got a favor to ask," it means he's about to lay the biggest favor in the world on you.

"Former president Clinton and I have struck up a friendship," he explained. "I thought it might be fun to spend some time together, out of public view, just enjoying each other's company, playing some golf, and having some nice dinners. We were exploring the idea of doing a little vacation getaway together, but it turns out it's easier to just have him up to Walker's Point in Kennebunkport."

"Okay, sir," I said.

"Here's my favor, then," he continued. "We both agreed it would be nice to have a third person there, who is not in the world of politics, who can be our so-called intermediary — there to keep the conversation going and make sure it never deviates into politics or world issues. Just someone we can have some fun with."

I said, "Yes, sir."

"The favor is we've both decided you should be the guy," he said. "I really need you to come up to Maine to spend a couple of days with us this summer."

In the quiet of my speechlessness, President Bush continued. "We're just a couple of old, retired presidents. Your schedule is much busier than ours. We need to work this around you." (Which I thought was truly comical.) "Could you possibly choose some dates you would be available?"

The "favor" President Bush asked me for was an opportunity for me, at dates of my choosing, to spend a couple of days with two former presidents playing golf, taking boat rides, and eating lobster in beautiful seaside Kennebunkport, Maine.

That's George Bush.

President Clinton had scheduled a book signing in nearby Portland, Maine, to get himself up into the area. (Portland is an Atlantic seaport about twenty miles north of Kennebunkport.)

President Bush suggested that, instead of Clinton being driven from Portland to Kennebunkport, he would pick him up and bring him to the house via his speedboat *Fidelity*.

Jim Nantz, a friend who'd been invited by the president, was on board as the president pointed the boat out into the open ocean and headed east with a Secret Service flanker boat shadowing along. Tom Frechette, the president's personal aide, helped navigate, along with a Secret Service agent, on what Nantz subsequently described as a "really nasty, stormy day." One of those nor'easters was blowing in, so it was cold and rainy and sizable waves were breaking in the Atlantic. *Fidelity*, and those aboard, got tossed around as they pounded and plowed along the coast. Frechette was a gifted mariner, and between him and the president they had all the instruments they needed, but they could not see anything because the fog layer was so low.

They were at sea for about forty minutes when they started looking at the radar and determined it was time to turn into an inlet. They cut back the engines, and Nantz was able to overhear all the alternating communication on the radios between the Secret Service agent on board and the Clinton detail:

"#42 is two minutes out . . . over."

"#41 is just entering the harbor . . . over."

"#42 is one minute out . . . over."

"#41 . . . one minute out . . . over."

"42 . . . standing on dock in orange shirt . . . over."

"#41 looking for anything in a harbor shrouded with fog. Can't see anything . . . over."

All of a sudden, through the poor visibility, the president could make out something orange in the fog.

"Look, over there!" the president said, pointing.

Sure enough, standing on the edge of the dock, was President Clinton.

The engines were cut back and the boat gently idled up to dock.

Nantz remembers the fog enshrouded the secret rendezvous as if the scene were something out of a spy thriller movie. Here were two former world leaders meeting at some predetermined pier in Maine.

President Bush jumped out of the boat and got onto the pier, where the two presidents had a nice, warm hug. They were both giddy about how they'd pulled this off with no media cameras or fanfare. They both realized, without saying it, this was like something you'd see in the movies. You don't expect either former president to be able to maneuver in total anonymity.

"How was it getting up here?" President Clinton asked.

President Bush answered, "It was pretty bumpy. The seas were turbulent. Low ceiling. But it's no problem, we can handle it."

"George, I'm not sure it's a good idea we go back by boat then," Clinton said. He'd recently had a heart procedure of some sort. He was concerned about all the jostling going back on the boat over the waves.

With that, both presidents looked around at one of the lead agents on the shore, from President Clinton's detail. They wondered if there was enough room to go back by car. One of the vehicles had already been released, so there wasn't the usual mobile support motorcade you would expect with two former presidents hitting the road.

"Sir, we can call for a backup vehicle to come back and assist," the agent offered.

"No, no let's just go back by car," said President Bush. He flipped the boat keys to Frechette and asked him to pilot *Fidelity* back to Walker's Point. The remaining men piled into the lone Suburban. An agent was driving, and another agent was sitting in front. The second row was a bench seat with the two presidents and Nantz squeezed onto it.

After a day spent by air, sea, and land, President Bush decided to gather a small group and take President Clinton out to dinner in Kennebunkport at Stripers Waterside Restaurant. Stripers is on Ocean Avenue near where the ocean meets the Kennebunk River. The fresh seafood restaurant has a waterside deck with sunset views and a New England–style dining room.

Into Stripers walked the two former presidents; former first lady Barbara Bush; their daughter Doro Bush; Jim Nantz; Laura Graham and Jean Becker, who were, respectively, President Clinton's and Bush's chiefs of staff; and Doug Band, who was a personal aide to President Clinton. The shock on the other diners' faces as this parade of notables quietly filed in and sat down must have been priceless!

At Mrs. Bush's recommendation, Nantz stood and delivered a toast to the fact that two former political rivals had become friends, showing the rest of the world what democracy really is all about and what America, as a country, represents. Nantz noted that though Americans may not agree on everything philosophically, if the two of them could get along and truly enjoy each other's friendship that should be a lesson to everyone. It was the launch of two special days.

President Clinton stayed two nights, and I joined the presidents and Nantz for a couple of rounds of golf.

We had the two Secret Service pods—one for President Bush and one for President Clinton—moving about the property at Cape Arundel. I was a busy golf professional that day preparing for their arrival. When their motorcade of SUVs did turn up, I had to switch hats to "player," and "host," since they'd asked me to join them. It was sometimes very demanding to go out there and try to play well—to the expected level of a golf professional—while trying to keep an eye on the operation with a million things going on. Thanks to a great staff and an understanding membership, these events went very smoothly and became part of our club's long history.

On our way to the first tee, some press turned up with cameras hoping for an interview. During the president's term in office a designated access point was provided for the media to congregate to cover the president so they would not be running all over the property and the president could enjoy his round. There was another access point for them at the ninth green and beside the eighteenth hole so they could speak to the president after his round. There were plenty of photo opportunities for them at those points.

The presidents spoke briefly to the media about working together as a team for tsunami relief and they discussed their common passion, despite their opposing political philosophies, to help the world and to serve and help people in need.

Nantz and I were thrilled to be involved, and the club was very proud to have yet another president at Cape Arundel. I rode in the cart with Nantz and the two presidents rode together. We had a gallery walking and enjoying the opportunity to experience historic, presidential golf in Maine. President Clinton played some very nice golf, making birdies on the second and third holes. He was two-under-par after three holes—quite the statement! It was a great start, but it was hard to maintain. Eventually he hit some balls behind trees and into some of the deep fescue grass that gave the course its golden, classic definition but challenged him. He was frustrated a couple of times because he didn't know the course and some of his shots left his ball in some precarious positions, which, of course, was never his fault. I remember he topped a shot one time and commented he didn't know the yardage and had used the wrong club.

Some of our members who were Democrats came out to watch some golf for the very first time. President Clinton, famous for "working the rope line," was at it that day, greeting people who'd lined the holes to watch and catch a glimpse of him. He'd chat with them all for a bit, which made our round slower than normal. President Bush had to call Walker's Point and tell them to hold lunch!

As I recall, Clinton wasn't feeling all that well that day, but #42 endured all the way through the round. We had a fun match, everyone hit good shots, and the game of golf was the winner.

There was a lot of ribbing, laughing, reading greens, and missing putts, like any four guys who were knocking the ball around. I think President Clinton hit three tee shots on the seventeenth hole, but no one minded since this gathering was so good for the game of golf.

I remember that "Team Bush and Raynor" were victorious in the match over "Team Clinton and Nantz," so the home team won, so to speak. More importantly, the game and sport won and benefitted from the news accounts of two former rivals peacefully playing golf.

Paul Marchand, Director of Golf at The Summit Club, Celebrity Golf Coach, and Past President's Cup Vice-Captain

In 1995 the president invited my wife Judy and me, along with our oldest daughter Morgan, who was about four years old, to come to Kennebunkport for the first time. We ended up making the trip there about twelve years in a row. The visits would generally be about three days and two nights. We'd play about two or three rounds of golf at Cape Arundel with Ken Raynor and have dinner or go out on the president's boat Fidelity.

We felt right at home as many of the other Bush Family members were there, too, including Governor George W. Bush.

The next year, in 1996, back in Houston, the Bushes invited us to a Houston Astros baseball game at the Astrodome, before which, of course, he threw out the ceremonial first pitch. My wife Judy and I and President and Mrs.

Bush were in the limousine, sitting in the seats facing each other, on the way home when the president said, "You all need to make your dates to come back to Kennebunkport this summer. Would you like to bring someone with you?"

I thought about it for a moment, looked at my wife, and answered, "I'd love to bring my college buddies Jim Nantz and Freddie Couples. They'd love to see your beautiful home and enjoy the fun we've been having there."

"Then you should invite them and their wives," President Bush said.

Later that summer, sure enough, we made a trip up there to Maine together. We had a fabulous time.

Couples had met the president briefly when he went to the White House as a member of the Ryder Cup team for a photo-op in the Oval Office. To be in their home though at Walker's Point was a treat. Couples, being the PGA Tour star he is, shot the Cape Arundel course record of 62 while I shot 65. There was a lot of photo-taking going on, and we were all posing, when suddenly the president jabbed me.

"Will the guy who shot 65 please move over so I can have my photo taken with the guy who shot 62?" President Bush joked. We all laughed.

Later that evening at his home on Walker's Point, the president said, "I've been asked to go into town to get a pizza for the grandkids. Would you like to go?"

Of course Couples and I agreed, and to my surprise we boarded his boat, which he was very proud of. He likes to drive the boat very fast, which is exciting. The Secret Service agent, a wonderful guy named Jimmy Rogers, was a golf nut and having a lot of fun with Couples being on board.

When we were closing in on town, President Bush slowed the engines and we tethered the boat to the dock. We then got ready to climb up the ladder and walk into town to a little store to get the pizza, when Couples asked Rogers, "President Bush isn't really going to climb up there and go into town to pick up a pizza, is he?"

Rogers said, "Oh yeah. He'll do that."

"Why don't you let me go do that?" Couples offered. "I'll go get the pizza."

In the company he was in, Couples, who is used to being the recognizable star, was reduced to offering to be the more anonymous pizza runner.

Rogers insisted, though, "The president likes doing it. He'll be fine."

Sure enough we followed behind the president and we went into the little shop and there were three or four tables of people enjoying dinner in Kennebunkport. He shocked everybody when he showed up. The people were aghast as he went to several of the tables and greeted the families and tapped the kids on the heads.

"I hope you're having a good time," he asked the tourists as they shook his hand and posed for quick photos.

Couples and I were taking all this in and, for once, nobody seemed to fuss over the great Freddie "Boom Boom" Couples (which, believe me, was fine with Fred)!

When the president got to the counter, he greeted the owner and traded comments about their families. Then President Bush put his wallet on the counter and asked. "What's it going to be? How much do I owe you?"

"This one's on us, Mr. President."

"No, no," President Bush insisted. "What do I owe you?"

The president eventually paid in cash, put his wallet back in his pocket, carried the pizza himself, and turned around and said goodbye to everyone in the store as we left.

We went back down the ladder into the boat and Couples was smiling and shaking his head. I thought about how every professional athlete should see how President Bush went through his daily life, quickly engaged with people, and kept on track, too.

It wasn't just on *Fidelity* that the president's plans have been hampered by the fog. On another occasion, in 1995, we were fishing in Newfoundland and were traveling via helicopter. The two choppers were taking our small group from our lodging to the Long Harbour River to go salmon fishing. While in the air, we encountered an extremely heavy fog bank. The chopper pilots were not comfortable flying though the heavy fog, let alone doing it

FISHING, *FIDELITY*, AND FUN   **125**

with a former president of the United States on board. We had two choppers flying, and both pilots agreed they should put down, so we did.

"If the fog lifts, we can continue our trip," one of the pilots advised us.

In the meantime, while we waited, the president was impatient, so he was walking around outside the chopper and fell into a deep bog. The seventy-one-year-old was up to his hips in the bog and could not get out. He might have drowned in there had not the Secret Service agents, once hearing someone cry, "The president is down!" hustled over and urgently pulled the president out of the bog after a ten-minute struggle.

"I wouldn't be truthful if I didn't indicate he could have been in a serious situation. Within seconds he was up to his armpits. It was a matter of a few more seconds until he would have been in over his head," Craig Dobbin, our host, who owned the helicopter, told the Canadian Press.

President Bush was barely rattled by what happened. He wanted to get on with the fishing.

Johnny Morris, CEO of Bass Pro Shops

We were in Newfoundland fishing for Atlantic salmon in remote rivers. Ken Raynor and I were being flown to a river in a helicopter while President Bush was in another. It got so foggy we had to set down. Ken and I caught up with the president later and the Secret Service agents were shaking their heads. While the president's chopper was grounded by the fog, he had to go off to take a break and find a bush to answer "Mother Nature's Call."

When he didn't come back for quite a while, the Secret Service agents began to worry. They didn't want to be rude or intrusive of his "bathroom break," but they could not wait any longer, so a US Secret Service Agent and Canadian Mounted Policeman went to see what was taking so long.

They found that the president has inadvertently stepped into a bog and was sunk up to his chin! He was, literally, bogged down! The agents said the reason they were able to save President Bush was that he remained very calm. He didn't even carry on about it.

When the fog finally lifted, it didn't lift in a direction that helped us. It remained an obstruction to getting to the river we were headed to—the

Long Harbour — but it lifted in the direction of Gander. The Gander River is very well known as a great river to fish. It's where the famous Gander boats, which are like long, square canoes, originated. So after a few quick phone calls, we altered the plan and quickly got back into the whirly birds. Within thirty minutes we descended upon a fishing camp in Gander.

A woman came out to greet us and had the fish camp staff rustle up some guides for us. The next thing she knew she was sitting in her lovely home on the Gander River having breakfast with someone she just unexpectedly met — the former president of the United States!

The camp found four or five Gander boats for us to go down the river to fish for Atlantic salmon for most of the rest of the afternoon. By then, luckily, the fog lifted and we were able to fly back to our cabins.

It seemed like we were gone just as fast as we'd arrived.

Dave Hall, Former Director of the Fish and Wildlife Service Under President George W. Bush and Current CEO of Ducks Unlimited
Under the leadership and direction of President George H. W. Bush, the United States established for the first time the policy of "No Net Loss of Wetlands," which directed that any wetlands newly affected by draining or development must be offset by the creation or improvement of another wetland of the same size and function. Through that directive alone, a potential loss of hundreds of thousands of wetlands have been avoided, mitigated, or replaced across this great nation.

During his presidency, fifty-six new National Wildlife Refuges were established, more than President Theodore Roosevelt — who is seen as the father of the National Wildlife Refuge System — had established (fifty). These refuges have conserved more than three million acres of wild places for future generations to enjoy.

For almost ten years, President Bush, Johnny Morris, and I went up to New-foundland as guests of Dobbin, who was chairman of the CHC Helicopter Corporation (the world's largest chopper corporation), and his wife Elaine. Dobbin loved fishing, and when he got into the helicopter business, he was able to combine the two passions.

We'd fly in helicopters, over the Caribou herds and fly low-profile up these world-renowned, amazing, pristine rivers. One of the rivers was called the Adlatok. It's about 250 kilometers long, stretching from Quebec to the Labrador coast. Dobbin had built a lodge up there on sprawling, natural land he'd leased for ninety-nine years. The lodging was beautiful and, for being a few hundred miles north of Goose Bay in the middle of nowhere, Dobbin had done an incredible job with it. It was a four-bedroom log cabin, all shellacked, with hardwood floors and leather couches. There was a full bar and a waitstaff, cooks, and a mechanic—about twenty people on staff—who stayed in an adjoining cabin and tent. Guests there lived high on the hog in the middle of absolutely nowhere. All the electricity was via genera-tors. All the cooking was propane. All the refrigeration was propane. Heli-copters flew things in and it was otherwise self-sufficient and only open a few months each year during fishing season.

It all started when the Canadian government was trying to buy up all the commercial licenses to protect Atlantic salmon in Canadian waters. A lot of the natives who lived in these remote areas had nets in the rivers to make a living catching salmon. Atlantic salmon do not die like western species do. The western salmon, they come up and spawn and die, like the sockeye salmon. The Canadian government wanted to protect the fish. They wanted to show that the locals could still make a living recreational fishing if the fishing were good enough and they weren't killing the Atlantic salmon in the nets in the river before they spawned. They allocated millions of dollars to buy the licenses from the natives and give them some money to stop net fishing and encourage recreational fishing as an alternative revenue source.

One of the ways the Canadian government wanted to promote recre-ational fishing in the area was to have a well-known celebrity come to Can-ada as a recreational fisherman. Our US Conservation Department, Fish and Game, contacted Johnny Morris from Bass Pro Shops. Morris got President Bush involved, and he invited me.

Morris flew to Kennebunkport, and Dobbin, our host for the trip, whom we were meeting for the first time, brought his own plane to pick us up. We had a wonderful dinner at Walker's Point and they stayed the night. We all got along great—it was like we'd known Craig forever, and we were all eager to go fishing. Little did I know this was the first of an adventure that would take place each summer for the next decade.

The next morning, we were up early and at dawn boarded Dobbins's beautiful airplane bound for the military base at Goose Bay. The next thing we knew, we're in choppers soaring over this incredible Labrador landscape of tundra, granite peaks, and icebergs. The wind was blowing, and we viewed the mouth of the Adlatok River where the water goes from salt to fresh, and that's where Dobbin had built this beautiful cabin that we would be calling home for three nights.

Lee Wulff, a famous, pioneering, world-record-holding fly fisherman, was born in Alaska and created very popular dry flies. He was also an author, a lecturer, and a filmmaker, and he was on record as saying his favorite river in all of Labrador in which to fish for Atlantic salmon was the Adlatok. And there we were.

Susan Biddle, the White House photographer, flew in, and Dobbin had some friends who were there to meet the president, including a couple of Canadian provincial governors. Television reporter Paula Zahn wanted to do a feature on the president, so, on one of our annual trips, he agreed to do it, and told her it might be fun if she came to Adlatok with us to do a candid piece. The president knew this kind of publicity could help tourism in the region. So she came up and interviewed President Bush in the cabin on camera, but she also put on some waders and got in the river and fished side by side with us. The president talked with her while he casted. I tried to teach her how to cast some. (I remember he made television reporter Jamie Gangel do the same thing once, standing in the mud and casting off the bank of the Kennebunk River behind Cape Arundel.)

Baseball legend Ted Williams was supposed to go our first year, but he had to cancel the night before we left. It was funny because we all had baseballs in our suitcases for him to sign! Williams was one of the great fly fishermen of all time. Supposedly he'd caught two thousand salmon, two thousand bonefish, and two thousand tarpon on fly before anyone else ever had.

No matter who was there, we all hung around in our fishing clothes and waders. We were there to fish and have wonderful dinners and great conversations. It was all about entertainment. We'd spend the whole day in the river and we could do whatever we wanted. I had my own helicopter pilot when I wanted to find a new spot on the river to fish with my guide. Dobbin and the president did a lot of fishing side by side, as I did with Morris. We'd stop and watch each other when someone hooked into a fish. We'd release most of the salmon, but one or two, with tags, we kept for photos or dinner.

Some days we'd fly in the choppers to a different river and fish there all day to experience the area's pure but varied beauty and in pursuit of a trophy fish.

I just loved witnessing the president's joy in the strike of a fish and fight to catch a fresh salmon from the sea. I loved the sound of the drag as the fish ripped the line from #41's reel. It's a sensation we still talk about to this day.

We often used a Blue Charm salmon fly, which originated in the early 1900s in Scotland. Scotsman Arthur Wood reportedly caught thirty-five hundred salmon with these on the River Dee in Aberdeenshire. The Blue Charm is famous in Labrador and was the only fly the guides would even let us use up there, only occasionally substituted by the "Bomber"/"Green Machine." A Blue Charm is tied with a body of black floss, ribbed with silver or gold tinsel, a throat of blue hackle feathers, and wings of mallard and teal feathers.

A guide favorite in Labrador. (*Photo by Havard Eide*)

At the end of the day we took the helicopters out and landed on an iceberg. I learned you don't technically "land" on an iceberg because it can be unstable and very slippery. So the "bird" keeps its blades going at full speed even though the rudders are touching the ice. We got out of the chopper very carefully and broke off a chunk of ice and put it in the cooler. It was basically two-thousand-year-old ice, because it had been frozen that long before it broke off as an iceberg and floated in the sea. And that two-thousand-year-old ice, which we ventured to procure, is what we drank our cocktails on that night! Talk about decadent. Iceberg ice! Here we were having Crown Royal or Irish whiskey on two-thousand-year-old ice cubes, toasting our many friends.

The evenings were beautiful. We'd see the stars and watch the Northern Lights with no light pollution to obscure them since there's not a single town for two hundred miles.

When you're up all day fishing in the river and working hard, you don't stay up late. We'd have a tremendous dinner and great wine and conversation. We'd talk about the fish that got away or maybe do some work on the reels if it was needed. On occasion, Dobbin would have a musician flown in by helicopter so we'd hear some guitar or electric piano with singers and an outside bonfire lighting up the evening sky.

Those trips provided an escape for everyone involved. And what a unique assignment for the Secret Service agents. It was so outside the ordinary for them, but being on the Bush detail changed all that! During the downtime in the rotation for the agents, when they were off duty, some of them would have an opportunity to use the choppers and catch fish of their own. The president loved knowing that they had a chance to enjoy this opportunity.

George Bush being in Labrador was big news, and it made headlines in some of the Labrador newspapers because we were there with the idea of helping the Canadian government with securing the commercial fishing licenses. There were a couple of First Nation people who lived on the river, in the middle of nowhere. One day one of the chiefs who also lived on the river in a house about a mile away told Dobbin he wanted to meet "this George Bush guy." Dobbin, in an effort to appease this neighbor, asked the president if he could bring him over. President Bush, an expert at such diplomacy, agreed.

The agents watched carefully and closely, and when they met, it was obvious the chief had been drinking. He gave the president a big kiss! Everyone was surprised because we thought he'd be upset that a US president was invading his land to fish his river. Dobbin was in shock, but our fishing president showed his excellent people skills and laughed it off—much to our host's relief and appreciation.

The Adlatok River now has a presidential plaque on a rock saying, "The Presidential Pool" . . . United States President George H. W. Bush Stood Here on This Rock and Fished for Atlantic Salmon. It's a great spot!

President Bush received an invitation in 1995 from Peter Pocklington, who owned the National Hockey League's very successful Edmonton Oilers, to come fishing in the Arctic. He'd invited others, including Glen Sather, who'd coached his team to four Stanley Cup titles; Harry Sinden, who'd coached and managed the Boston Bruins; Gary Bettman, the NHL commissioner; and some Canadian provincial governors.

Jeb Bush, who later became Governor of Florida, was originally supposed to go, but something on his schedule prevented him from joining, so I got drafted. Part of my duties for the trip was to meet and escort Jeb's son, whom they refer to as "Jebbie," to California on a commercial flight to meet President Bush, who was already in the Golden State on business. Jebbie was about ten years old at the time, and I'd watched him grow up at the golf club and Walker's Point over the years.

Once in California, we stayed overnight at the home of a friend of President Bush, and the next morning I connected Jebbie with his "Gampy" and we got on board Pocklington's plane to fly north from San Francisco.

We had a beautiful flight over Mount St. Helens and Mount Rainier on the way to Yellowknife, the capital city of Canada's Northwest Territories, east of Alaska. If you've watched the television show *Ice Road Truckers*, you know the area because we were heading where those brave drivers originate from. From the Yellowknife Airport we were met by our hosts from Plummer's Lodges, who had our next aircraft ready for us: an old 1948 Douglas Skytrain DC-3. It was a great old propeller airplane that only flew about 180 miles per hour. The workhorse was white with a red stripe along it and had the words "Plummer's Lodges" painted over the door.

We boarded from the tarmac through a little stairway that unfolded out of the plane and flew a couple hours north in this big ol' plane.

It was a little louder inside than your typical private plane or commercial aircraft, so some of us hadn't noticed at first, but then a buzz went through the plane, when President Bush went up and assumed the co-pilot position in the cockpit. The president, who had been the youngest-ever naval aviator in the Second World War, was talking with the pilot, who I knew was honored to have him "second seat."

One of the pilots told me we'd flown for two hours over "land that man had never walked." That's how remote we were.

The president eventually yielded the co-pilot position so we could land on a very small, dirt strip at camp near Inuvik, 125 miles north of the Arctic Circle, to access the Tree River, which flows north into the Arctic Ocean. The Arctic has its own beauty in a very different way.

Our ultimate destination was an outpost camp along the Tree River. The only solid building at the outpost was the kitchen, where all the food supplies were. Every other structure, including our lodging, was just a wooden platform built over the permafrost with a canvas roof. Inside were plywood beds for four guys, each with a sleeping bag, and a potbelly stove in the middle. There were outhouses for when Mother Nature called. It's only open for six weeks each year (between July and August), and they get some snow every month of the year. It wasn't that cold, but it was damp due to the permafrost.

You might think these kinds of rugged accommodations might be beneath a former president, but President Bush loved it. He loved the fraternal camaraderie, the fishing trip, and just being one of the boys. He didn't mind roughing it one bit.

Plummer's Lodges has other facilities on Great Bear Lake and Great Slave Lake, with varying types of lodging, but their Tree River spot is gorgeously natural and has some of the greatest Arctic char fishing in the entire world. As a matter of fact, multiple Arctic char world records were set from this river. No one is sure why, but the Arctic char there are the biggest in the world. We'd catch fifteen- to twenty-pounders—beautiful fish sporting vibrant spawning colors of orange and pink with white trim on their fins—

with an eight-weight fly rod. Sometimes they had a green back or a silver back. They were just exquisite fish, and some of them had never been seen before by man or never seen a fly presented to them!

For three days we stayed in that outpost, fifteen feet from the roaring Tree River right at the beginning of the first "white water," meaning salt water below us from the rapids and fresh water above us. We could hike to the edge of the trail, and if we wanted to fish on the other side there was one big, long pool and a boat would motor us to the other side. We'd just hike the edge of either side of the river in our waders. It was muddy and dirty and all tundra. It could be a two-mile hike depending on where you wanted to fish the river, which we did multiple times each day. There were a couple of beautiful three- and four-foot waterfalls we couldn't imagine the fish could navigate—but they do. They don't jump like the Atlantic salmon do, but the char do have the power to swim up against the torrential flume of an angled fall. We'd stay out in that gorgeous natural setting a good portion of the day.

One of the days, the president and I had been fishing for what felt like the entire day. We were in awe and so glad to be there. At some point we had stopped for a nice streamside lunch with some fish the guides had cooked up fresh from out of the river. Because we were in the Arctic, there were no trees, so the only treelike plant you might see there in the permafrost is about the size of a mulberry bush. You can't collect wood like you could in the Rockies or almost any other river we might fish in New England, so in order to cook over a streamside fire, the guides had to carry in kindling and two-by-fours that they'd split up for firewood.

Fresh Arctic char off an open fire is one of the best fish you can eat. It's similar to a salmon but maybe even a little more tender. It comes from very cold water so it provides good, firm meat. We promote and enact conservation and enjoy catch and release fishing, but the experience requires eating at least one fresh fish, which we did.

To catch Arctic char, we used fly rods. You can catch them on spoons or spinners and rip it through the water. The char can be aggressive because they're coming in from the Arctic Ocean to spawn. We wore our waders so in some spots we stood in the river—but not very far in, because it's much too heavy of a current. You couldn't possibly stand in some of the torrents of clear water. We may have stood knee-deep in water sometimes, but we never went farther in than that. In catching the char, you're fighting the power of the river and the power of the twenty-plus-pound fish that survives in this frigid water, so you know they're products of their environment, which is a tough one. You can imagine how strong they are.

President Bush had a guide with him, and occasionally, on a back cast, the president's fly would catch on the rocks or a little bush behind him. The guide was nice enough to run back and untangle or free the fly from the rocks, so he earned the nickname "Rock Man" from the president. Following the trip the president sent him, along with all the others who'd worked so hard ensuring the success of our trip, an autographed photo signed to "Rock Man" with many thanks.

The afternoon ran by just as the river ceaselessly had.

"Ken, I'm going to head back to camp," President Bush finally told me.

"Well if you don't mind, sir, I am going to keep on fishing a little longer," I responded. He smiled, understanding the joy of it all, and made his way back.

My shoulder blades were on fire. I'd been fishing for hours and hours. I had a fishing vest on loaded with gear and so I just kept at it. Sometime later, I eventually walked back to camp and found everyone sitting around having appetizers and waiting for dinner to be served.

"Where've you been, Kenny?" someone asked me.

"I've been fishing, why?"

"Kenny, it's 10:30 at night!"

I would have sworn it was about six o'clock. I had forgotten we were in the land of the midnight sun, and during the summer it doesn't really get dark, just colder. Plus, I could barely believe I'd been fishing since 7:30 in the morning, almost without a break!

On one of those late nights after dinner, Gary Bettman and I decided to take a little aluminum boat and go downriver with a guide and actually see the Arctic Ocean. We'd come that far, so it seemed like something we should do since we were there. We headed down the river and, because of the high humidity, the coldness was bone-chilling and damp. Bettman and I were dressed in overalls, many inner layers, and heavy coats, ski hats, and gloves. For some reason there had been a 1-iron golf club in the camp and a sleeve of three golf balls, so we'd thrown them into the boat. When the guide got us to the mouth of the river opening to the Arctic Ocean, it was midnight.

"Let's do it, Kenny," Bettman said. "Let's each hit a golf ball into the Arctic Ocean."

"I bet no one has ever done it with a 1-iron," I ventured, since the 1-iron is an almost nonexistent club.

"You can be the only PGA pro ever to hit a golf ball with a 1-iron into the Arctic," Bettman suggested.

Hockey's commissioner and I then took turns "growing the game" in the Arctic—by "exporting" golf balls via a 1-iron, into the deep, cold, vast sea at midnight.

Each night after dinner everyone would fall asleep quickly and be up early to fish all day once again.

The remote camp was peaceful, until one day when a surprise visitor ambled along: an Arctic grizzly bear, which is larger than your standard grizzly. It had a light-brown, almost blonde color of fur. The Secret Service estimated the giant, eighteen-hundred-pound beautiful animal as being three hundred to four hundred yards away from the camp and the president. The agents determined a visual "line in the sand" about two hundred yards out. If the bear crossed that line, it would not have been a good thing for the bear. Luckily the bear, which is endangered and protected in the Arctic, kept doing his own thing. It was an incredible sight. The president didn't seem bothered at all by the bear, as he was still loving the fishing.

The next day we were walking out in the scrub where the bear had been. What looked easy for the bear to walk on was tedious for us to traverse and took us a long time to get though. The bear had been walking on top of all the branches with its huge paws while we had to walk on earth. That indicated that if the bear had chased us, there would have been no way we were going to be able to get away from it on the terrain we were on.

I thought about the Secret Service agents who were assigned to protect the former president. They'd probably figured it was a comfortable job until one day they were staying up all night in the Arctic standing outside a tent hoping an eighteen-hundred-pound bear wasn't sizing them up! Not to mention the bugs and mosquitoes. Excessive duty!

We did some flying in a de Havilland Canada DHC-3 Otter floatplane, too, which was a seaplane that took us up to the Horton River. There we fished for Arctic grayling, another species of fish with a very large dorsal fin on it. We used five-weight fly rods for the grayling with tiny, rubber-legged flies. These Arctic grayling would come along and slurp them right off the surface. They don't run as large as the char; they're twelve to twenty inches compared to the twenty-five-pounders we had been catching.

President Bush and I were standing side by side in a little pool fishing, and we looked over to see these little scrub bushes. Sticking out from behind them were the heads of four reindeer. I was pinching myself the entire time because from the floatplane we also spotted some musk oxen, which are five feet tall, eight-hundred-pound, shaggy-haired, Arctic herd animals with dramatically curved horns.

By the end of the trip, everyone's nicknames had been established, and Mr. Pocklington gave each of us a jacket with our nicknames embroidered on them.

My nickname was "Scratch," since I was a PGA professional with therefore, presumably, a "scratch" (zero) handicap.

Ambassador Ken Taylor was "007" because he was the Canadian ambassador to Iran who harbored American Embassy workers who escaped the militant takeover in 1979 and eventually avoided being hostages by escaping Iran.

Glen Sather was "Slats."

Harry Sinden was "Northern Dancer."

Gary Bettman was "Commish."

Mr. Pocklington was "HRM Puck."

The president's nickname was, of course, "Commander in Chief."

It's kind of fun to know that both of his beloved fishing escapes—Tree River in the Arctic and the Adlatok River in Labrador—each have a plaque stating something to the effect that George H. W. Bush, the 41st president of the United States, fished here. For generations the other hearty fishermen who make the trek to those remote locations in his footsteps will enjoy seeing those plaques.

In subsequent years, Johnny Morris, the founder of Bass Pro Shops, and Bob Rich, who owned Rich's Products, a giant food supply corporation out of Buffalo (the Bills' NFL football stadium is named for his company), were invited to participate in the Tree River experience, as was Andy Mill, host of an outdoor television show. While on that trip, Andy filmed and produced a thirty-minute television special of the trip.

President Bush and I still talk about the Tree River, and he tells me it may be his favorite place he's ever been. One of his prized possessions is that mounted Arctic char he caught there. It's in his office today in Kennebunkport, and it reminds him about the adventures he had over the years while still hearing the sound of the reel "singing" on the fishes' first run! The ability for him, at his age and with his demanding life's experiences, to live out a wildlife adventure with others who understood the pure joy of letting their collective hair down and just being fishermen and "guys," was something President Bush treasured.

In June 2014, Johnny Morris, to celebrate President Bush's ninetieth birthday, brought some friends to Kennebunkport to go fishing with #41 once again. After a morning of fishing off the Atlantic coast, Morris honored the president with the Bass Pro Shops Lifetime Conservation Achievement Award and a $125,000 gift in the president's name to the Recreational Boating and Fishing Foundation.

"President Bush is a remarkable man who has had an immeasurably profound, positive impact on our nation's fish and wildlife resources. He is a passionate fisherman and sportsman whose well-known love of fishing has made him one of the best ambassadors the sport of fishing has ever had," Morris said.

They reminisced about the trips to Newfoundland and Labrador, the Arctic, and the times they spent bass fishing in Alabama, trout fishing in the Ozarks, the River Test in England, and striper fishing right there in Maine.

Jeff Trandahl, executive director and CEO of the National Fish and Wildlife Foundation, phoned in to the gathering to announce a partnership to provide a one million dollar gift to the new President George H. W. Bush Conservation Fund.

Mike Nussman, president and CEO of the American Sportfishing Association, awarded the inaugural Keep America Fishing Lifetime Achievement Award to President Bush and named it after him.

George Dunklin Jr., the president of Ducks Unlimited, brought a beautiful gift of waterfowl art; and Matt Connolly, president of the Bonefish and

Tarpon Trust, really surprised the president by renaming the Florida Keys' "Little Basin" to "Two Georges Flat" in honor of President Bush and his late friend and legendary fishing guide George Hommell Jr.

Tom Bradbury, executive director of the Kennebunkport Conservation Trust, was there, and sometimes I cannot believe it, but I was there, too, witnessing a touching moment for the president, who was greatly honored. I am sure, though, the president felt the joy of remembering many of his life's fishing experiences and how much excitement and peace the sport had given him. Knowing his humility, I am sure he felt fishing gave his soul more than he ever could have given back.

8

MISSIONS DEFINED AND MISSIONS COMPLETED

In Kenne-Bush-Port, as some in the media had taken to calling Kennebunkport, a simple drive over to the beach, when it included the president of the United States, meant a motorcade of a black limousine, three four-wheel-drive utility vehicles with flashing lights, a State Police cruiser, two vans full of media people and reporters, an ambulance, and more.

It was not unlike the president to stop the motorcade occasionally to talk to someone. He has, for instance, stopped at Patten's Berry Farm near Cape Arundel Golf Club just to thank the owners for sending him some berries. It can be amusing to see how surprised people are when the president wheels in. I suppose when they sent a gift they did not expect a personal visit in return from the world's most prolific note-writer.

The stories are endless. On another occasion, President Bush stopped his motorcade through Kennebunkport to surprise a newlywed couple riding in a carriage!

Simply taking a walk, especially during his presidency, was not as simple as it sounds. Though some calories were definitely burned during eighteen holes at Cape Arundel, the president liked to walk without hitting a golf ball too, so off-season I would get a call inviting me to go power-walking with him. Sometimes it would be after church on Sunday morning—no matter how cold or windy it was. I'd dress in layers and drive over to his Walker's Point home and we'd jump into the limousine and the motorcade would take us over to Parson's Beach or Goose Rocks Beach.

Goose Rocks Beach is north of Walker's Point, on Kings Highway, beyond Cape Porpoise. It's three miles long and wide, with the sand protected by the "Goose Rocks" barrier reef. Parson's Beach is another long sandy beach, in the other direction off Route 9, between Wells and Kennebunkport, adjacent to the Rachel Carson Preserve.

On the walks, which were brisk, we would talk about fishing, family, and golf. Was I hoping that on our walks President Bush, the former United Nations ambassador and CIA director, would spill the beans on what really happened at Area 51 or maybe a state secret of some sort? Well, it was simply more like two guys taking a walk on the weekend to get out of the house and shoot the breeze. In fact, the president once joked if he didn't go out for a walk Mrs. Bush would have found something for him to do around the house.

Not that he was above chores. He approached them with the same enthusiasm as any of the many activities that took place when he was at his "vacation home." *USA Today* once reported that he was raking and bagging yard debris after a fireworks display—and that was before a day of jogging, swimming, boating, and golf—in between phone calls with various prime ministers and kings.

There were a few days it was about 18 degrees with the wind blowing off the ocean. His intent was to walk hard enough to work up a sweat, and to get his springer spaniel Ranger out there with him. We walked at a pace just short of a jog, and if it were not for the cameras and media entourage following, no one in the homes on the beach or watching from a distance would have even known it was the president bundled up out there in a big parka, Russian fur cap, and gloves power-walking in the wind. They were special, quiet moments—"just the two of us," with the Secret Service, his staff, and the media, of course!

I remember a more serious occasion, though, during which it was about 10 degrees outside in mid-February . . . but the power walk was still on. Parson's Beach was the location this time, and the president walked faster than normal with the intent of breaking a sweat. In the cold he wore tennis shoes, a red winter coat and scarf, and one of those trapper-style winter hats with the flaps that fell down over his ears. He carried a walking stick. President Bush had a great deal on his mind. One month earlier he'd ordered the Desert Storm coalition air war against Saddam Hussein's Iraq in order to force the end of their invasion of neighboring Kuwait.

On the motorcade ride from Walker's Point to the beach, President Bush noticed all of the American flags waving from people's homes in support. He was very appreciative of the patriotism.

Within days of our walk, the ground war portion of the coalition operation would begin, which certainly the president must have known when we dragged his aides and the media members out along the angry Atlantic shoreline.

I am not sure if President Bush had an inkling of just how successful the ground campaign would be or if he could have imagined that it would result in Iraq's withdrawal from Kuwait after only a few days.

As normal and regular as it seemed, I was reminded it was not just two pals out for a walk when I saw the resulting *York County Coast Star* newspaper headline: RAYNOR TAKES A WALK WITH THE PRESIDENT.

Susan Flood's story included a photo of the two of us walking and talking. The caption read: " . . . the two primarily discussed golfing and fishing." And yes, while we did talk about using barbless fishing hooks and the conservational benefits of promoting "catch and release" fishing, I was quoted in the story as saying, "[The president] is pretty confident the war is going to end soon."

Not long after that chilly walk on Parsons Beach, Anne and I, on our way down to Florida, were up on the residence level having a cocktail with Mrs. Bush. Her husband was about to arrive back from his day "at the office" — the Oval Office.

Upon his arrival, we went into his private office to watch the television news and share a little about our days with each other. The president, typically, might tell us about someone interesting he met or some other unique activity he was involved in. Each in its own way reflected his deep commitment to America, while he was still interested in our day — typical George Bush!

We made our way to the beautiful Jacqueline Kennedy Dining Room, just off the kitchen, where just the four of us sat down for dinner.

It was then that President Bush, our friend, stood up and broke the news.

"I'd like to propose a toast," he said, lifting his glass. "Here's to the ceasefire that will be announced in Operation Desert Storm tomorrow at 10:00 a.m."

It was another dose of reality of who my friend really is. It was an emotional moment. Kuwait had been freed, and the war was over.

Anne's brother Chuck Forrest was a Merchant Marine sea captain. In fact, he captained one of the first ships into Kuwait City after Desert Storm. He brought a mobile hospital in through the Suez Canal.

On one occasion Captain Chuck was in Germany with one of his fellow mates on a ship. They were reading while waiting for the ship to be unloaded at the dock. One of the fellows knew that Chuck was from Kennebunkport, so he held up the front page of the *Stars and Stripes* newspaper for him to see. On it was a photo of President Bush in a golf cart.

"Hey, Chuck, here's a picture of President Bush back in Maine," he pointed out.

Chuck looked over and got a big grin on his face when he saw the photo. "Yeah," he replied, "and the guy next to him is my brother-in-law!"

While it was flattering, on that occasion, to be seen in the media, another appearance in the press was less so. During President Bush's term in office, in August of 1990, I played golf with #41 and his son George W., who, as we now know, went on to become governor of Texas and president of the United States. Press photographers snapped away. The Associated Press released a photo for use in publications across the world featuring the president and his son, each in Texas Rangers caps, and both seen clutching putters and visibly wincing. The photo's caption read: "ANGUISHING OVER MISSED PUTT — President Bush and his son George react as golf pro

Ken Raynor just misses a putt during a game at the Cape Arundel Golf Club in Kennebunkport."

Can you imagine the embarrassment? Oh, why could the Bushes not have been photographed "smiling in jubilation over a putt sunk by golf pro Ken Raynor?" I imagine the officials at the PGA of America headquarters in Palm Beach Gardens had a good laugh at that one . . . or buried their heads in their hands!

I got redemption, though, for PGA professionals everywhere, on Saturday, August 2, 2002. A Reuters photo appeared, above the fold, right smack in the center of the front page

(AP photo/Doug Mills)

of the *New York Times* Sunday edition. The photo shows three men playing golf—a type of photo unheard of for the front page photo! And the vaunted Sunday edition! It was outstanding publicity for the sport we love and for PGA professionals everywhere. This time the caption read: "President Bush and his father and the club pro Ken Raynor played the 10th hole yesterday at the Cape Arundel Golf Club in Kennebunkport, ME. The President is staying at his parents' vacation house."

In the autumn after Desert Storm, in which coalition forces assembled by President Bush, including the US military, expelled the Iraqi invaders from Kuwait, a group had put together a charitable fundraising event to help the families of the troops and military reservists who had lost their incomes due to the war. The golf fundraiser was planned at Army Navy Country Club near Washington. President Bush had been asked to play in the event and participate, but due to other commitments, he just could not play. But to share the opportunity and try to help support the event, the president asked me if I could come down and participate on his behalf.

"Why don't you and Annie fly into Washington on Friday?" President Bush suggested. "We can spend the weekend at Camp David. Then we'll come back and play golf on Sunday, and then on Monday, you can participate in the event at Army Navy Country Club."

Of course we agreed. The original plan was we'd fly down from Maine into Washington, meet the Bushes at the White House, and fly, via the *Marine One* helicopter, from the White House to Camp David, the presidential retreat in Maryland. But it turned out on that Friday, the president's schedule allowed him to get out of Washington about forty-five minutes earlier than expected. So when we got off the plane in Washington, two White House stewards, in their jackets with the White House emblem on them, were waiting for us.

"The president has already departed for Camp David, Mr. Raynor," one of them informed us. "We're here to drive you to Camp David. The president is looking forward to your visit."

Camp David would only be a fifty-minute drive up into the Catoctin Mountain Park, in Frederick County, Maryland. The car had a telephone in it, which, through the White House operator, connected me directly to the president, who was already at Camp David.

"So sorry the plan changed a bit, Ken, but I hope everything has gone smoothly. You're on your way?" he asked.

I told him we were and how eager we were to see him and share what was going to be an exciting few days for us.

The Bushes spent every Christmas of his presidency at Camp David, and I believe that was so that the agents and staff who lived in the greater Washington, DC area could rotate home to be with their families during the holidays.

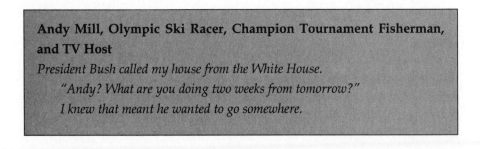

Andy Mill, Olympic Ski Racer, Champion Tournament Fisherman, and TV Host
President Bush called my house from the White House.
   "Andy? What are you doing two weeks from tomorrow?"
   I knew that meant he wanted to go somewhere.

It turned out he was going to give a speech in Aspen, Colorado, with British prime minister Margaret Thatcher. Thatcher's daughter Carol co-wrote my former wife Chris Evert's book about her championship tennis career, so we'd had opportunities to visit P.M. Thatcher at 10 Downing Street in London when Chrissie was competing at Wimbledon. President Bush knew this, so he thoughtfully asked if we'd like to join him and "Maggie" for dinner after their speech.

Of course we said yes, but then the phone rang again ten minutes later. It was President Bush calling back.

"Hey, what are you doing for the weekend? After the dinner why don't you fly back to Washington with me on Air Force One and we can take a helicopter up to Camp David for the weekend?"

This was the president of the United States making plans to hang out for the weekend! Of course we agreed.

When the weekend came, Chrissie and I received a call from the White House, while we were mid-flight to meet the president. We were advised that Kuwait had been invaded by Iraq and so President Bush would not be able to spend the night in Aspen, but he was still inviting us to come to Washington and go to Camp David. We diverted our plane to Dulles Airport, went to the White House, and spent the night in the Lincoln Bedroom.

Early in the morning we heard someone calling out in the hallway:

"Andy? Chrissie? Where are you guys?"

It was the unmistakable voice of President Bush, so we quickly presented ourselves and greeted him with a "good morning."

"C'mon over to the Oval Office about 3:00 p.m. I'll make a statement to the press and then we'll head over to Camp David."

That's exactly what we did, even though, given the world events and Iraq's invasion of Kuwait, there was a mini-summit of sorts at Camp David on Saturday. I shared a bite with him in the president's "Aspen Cabin." He never wanted to "talk shop" during meals, but I couldn't resist asking him what was going on with Kuwait. I'll never forget what he said.

"I cannot talk to Saddam Hussein. I can't negotiate with him," he answered. "My biggest regret is that we may go to war. But if we have to, we're going to do it right and it's not going to take very long."

"Oh my God," I thought to myself, "What did I just hear?"

Very early the next morning, about 6:00 a.m., there was a surprising knock on our cabin door. I climbed out of bed and cracked open the door to see President Bush's face.

"Hey, I can't sleep. Do you want to go shoot some skeet?"

I quickly got dressed and joined him in the dawn light. I realized that, once again, the leader of the free world was relying on his passion for the outdoors to bring some "space" to a serious situation.

Camp David, according to the White House, is formally known as the "Naval Support Facility Thurmont." It's been the official presidential retreat since President Franklin D. Roosevelt established it as such. After all, even if you are the president, would you want to spend your weekends living above the office in the middle of the city? It was President Eisenhower who changed the name from Shangri-La to "Camp David" in honor of his grandson.

Many world leaders have visited our presidents at the retreat, the first of which being Sir Winston Churchill. It was probably President Jimmy Carter, though, who brought the most attention to the residence when he held a summit there in 1978 between Israeli prime minister Menachem Begin and Egyptian president Anwar al-Sadat. They negotiated what became known as the "Camp David Accords."

You'll find it in the history books, but you won't find Camp David on a map. The Catoctin Mountain Park does not indicate the location for security and privacy reasons. It was dark when we were driven there, so I am not even sure I could find it again if I wanted to. Once through the gate, the car pulled up to one of the cabins in the pines, and, true to form, who was the first person standing there waiting to greet us? President Bush.

"Welcome to Camp David," he said with a smile, wanting to help us with our luggage. Anne and I arrived at this beautiful cabin and settled in after the drive. We looked at each other, realizing we were actually at Camp David. Walking through the tall pines, we pinched ourselves all the way to dinner.

After dinner, the president and first lady were excited because they were getting ready to watch an advance copy of an upcoming motion picture, taking advantage of one of the perks of our nation's highest office. They watched on a big, ten-foot screen that pulled down in the living room. There was a little hole amid the stones on the wall through which the film was projected onto the screen, not an amenity most homes have. We sat down to watch the movie *Shattered*, a mystery-drama starring Tom Berenger, Bob Hoskins, and Corbin Bernsen.

Fifteen minutes after the movie started, President Bush was snoring in his chair, asleep after what I presume was a long week being the leader of the free world.

"George! Go to bed!" Bar said, kicking him awake enough for her husband to stumble off to bed.

Not long after, Mrs. Bush fell asleep, too. She woke herself up, apologized, excused herself, and went to bed. We laughed at the thought of how many nights this happens in homes across America.

So here we were, Anne and I, sitting alone in the presidential cabin at Camp David, watching a movie before it was even released. We tiptoed out the door, walked to our cabin, and went to bed, excited about the days to follow.

There is no itinerary for visitors to Camp David. It's free and easy. So the next morning, on Saturday, we took a tour around the perimeter of the forested property. Guests can go on foot, pedal a bicycle, or ride on a golf cart—whatever they like. (President Gerald Ford liked to ride a snowmobile around the property.) There are winding paths up and down over the terrain and through the pines, which made for some brisk exercise and beautiful walks.

Nestled among these great pines was the president's office and conference meeting center. Many flags of the world surrounded an incredible conference table and, prominently displayed on the wall, hung the impressive Seal of the President of the United States etched in Waterford crystal.

In his working office, the president shared with us a statement of peace, presented to him by Soviet premier Mikhail Gorbachev. At first glance it simply was a map of the world, but the president then explained the relevance of the various lines and colored areas. It was really a copy of the plans the Soviet Union had during the Cold War era if they were ever to invade America! Gorbachev, who visited Camp David in June of 1990, presented it to President Bush during détente and the dissolution of the Soviet Union to underscore the sentiment they would never need those plans. I kept staring at in disbelief. It was chilling, and very, very real.

The office tour continued and every artifact shared had a special meaning. A cardboard cutout of the silhouette of a body from the chest up, like you'd see at a target range for practice, was propped up in the corner. It was full of bullet and knife holes and written in the top with magic marker were the words "Viva la Bush!" The president explained to me that it had been confiscated from the office of ousted Panamanian dictator Manuel Noriega. The troops, whom President Bush had directed into Panama on December 20, 1989 to capture and arrest Noriega, had discovered it and presented it to him after the invasion. Noriega, who had provoked the invasion by harassing US troops, fled his headquarters and sought refuge in a small, windowless room in the Embassy of the Holy See. US troops surrounded the embassy and played blaring rock music until Noriega finally emerged and surrendered after two weeks of the psychological warfare. Today both the map and the cutout are displayed at the Bush Library and Museum in College Station, Texas.

Much to my delight, there is golf at Camp David, thanks to President Dwight D. Eisenhower, who asked famed golf course architect Robert Trent Jones to build a green similar to one at Augusta National Golf Club and also reminiscent of that of Burning Tree Golf Club near Washington, DC. Tee shots, from near the president's Aspen Lodge, are from four different locations and about 100 to 150 yards to a single green guarded by a bunker. (It's been renovated some over the years.) It allowed for some fun family competitions through their many visits, and in true fashion we played some — yet another event for bragging rights!

That afternoon, the president wanted to get a little workout in before dusk, so we played "shirts and skins" wallyball, which is volleyball on a racquetball court. You can bounce the ball off the walls and send it careening all over the court. The game ended, with the president leading a jog back to the cabins, reminding all of us of his condition and commitment to stay in shape.

Sunday morning, we visited a very special chapel on the property. (The President and Mrs. Bush's daughter, Doro Bush, was married at Camp David.) The families of the Marines at Camp David and anyone else working there typically attend services, as do the president and his family, and any of their guests. It was filled to the brim with people. It was amazing how the president and Bar seemed to know everyone in attendance by name. The first couple gave the attendees and their children time and attention because the people were very important to them.

I remember the reverend spoke about faith and how you earn that faith. He brought up some of the children who were in the church and had them hanging from his extended arms with their feet off of the ground! He was trying to teach them, and us, about confidence and faith and relying on others. It made an impact on all of us in attendance.

I sat there, next to the president, with tears in my eyes as I looked around the room and saw a cross-section of America, with military families, staff, and friends—from the youngest child to the oldest adult—each being touched by the same inspirational message.

Then it was time to board *Marine One*, the helicopter that would take us back to Washington, DC, after a stop to play golf in Lake Manassas, Virginia. Typically the president boards first, but President Bush, since he was with friends, was escorting us and encouraging us to climb aboard.

After we'd all buckled in, the president nudged Anne.

"Watch this," he said, directing her to look out the window and explaining, "The moment the wheels of this chopper leave the ground, literally an inch off the ground, the color guard begins to take the presidential flag down."

We touched down in Lake Manassas, Virginia, for a round of golf at Robert Trent Jones Golf Club, which would be the site of the first-ever President's Cup matches in 1994. The biennial matches pit a team of professional golfers from the US PGA Tour against a team of pros from around the world (excluding Europe). The Robert Trent Jones Club has been the site of the matches four times, while other editions were contested in Australia, South Africa, South Korea, Canada, San Francisco, Columbus, and New Jersey, at Liberty National. The Robert Trent Jones Club, named after its architect, was brand new at the time.

Sportswriter Dan Jenkins joined us for the round in one of the two foursomes the president had gathered, while the first lady and Anne played in a two-ball on their own. Marvin Bush, the president's youngest son, had made the arrangements and joined the group to play. After nine holes, our two foursomes shuffled up players so everyone had a chance to play with the president.

After eighteen holes and handshakes with new friends, we boarded *Marine One* to fly back to Washington, DC, but due to an event taking place at the White House, we couldn't land the helicopter on the South Lawn, as is customary, so we landed at the Pentagon, instead. What a thrill for a golf pro from Maine riding *Marine One* with the president and landing on the Pentagon grounds, where there was security waiting with fire trucks and emergency vehicles on standby near the landing pad. Everything was "in case."

Once on the ground, we climbed into the presidential limousine and were White House–bound. The people on the sidewalks were excited to see the presidential motorcade pass by, so they were waving and taking photos. Anne, being so humble, felt uncomfortable waving, but everyone in the car was waving, and since the view through the windows is somewhat obscured, we told Anne she probably made some people happy thinking Barbara Bush waved back at them.

Seeing the flags on the front bumpers of the limousine made me realize I was living an experience I had always seen on television and never dreamed I would be any part of.

We arrived at the White House to walk right into a receiving line of celebrities who were going to play in the fundraising tournament. Jim Brown, John Daly, and others were there. As the president and Mrs. Bush went down the receiving line greeting these great athletes in the front lobby of the White House, in true Bush fashion, they took the time to introduce Anne and me to each guest.

The next morning a White House limousine took us to the golf fundraiser at Army Navy Country Club, which was just outside town in Virginia. Anne stayed for a while and then went to explore Washington. When the day was done, we both returned to the White House for a nice dinner with President and Mrs. Bush. Both were eager to hear all of the details about the fundraiser.

The next day, Anne and I flew back to Kennebunkport. I would say our "coach turned into a pumpkin," but our life in Kennebunkport is a peach, and we had been very inspired by the opportunity to be in the presence of the military and, in our small way, support them.

President Bush's experience with the military was something that has always interested me. President Bush talked here and there about the Second World War. Just before he'd turned nineteen years old, George Bush had become the Navy's youngest pilot. One year into his duty in the Pacific, the torpedo bomber he was flying, a TBM Avenger, was hit by anti-aircraft fire south of Japan. He was forced to bail from the aircraft and was rescued from a raft by a Navy submarine.

He'd hit his head while jumping then and wanted the chance to do it properly again, decades later. So President Bush did, and then famously also celebrated his seventy-fifth, eightieth, eighty-fifth, and ninetieth birthdays with recreational parachute jumps, somewhat to the concern of, but with the support of, the former first lady. George and Barbara Bush, wedded more than seventy years, have the longest marriage in presidential history. And she wanted to keep it that way!

It was in March of 1997, in Yuma, Arizona, that President Bush first jumped from an airplane by choice — for recreation and fulfillment. In doing so, he became the first American president ever to jump from an airplane. But it was the second time in his life he'd skydived. The first, of course, was fifty-two years earlier as a young aviator in combat. That same year Houston named its airport "George Bush Intercontinental Airport." There is a statue of the president, on the move, in the concourse.

In 1999, on the president's seventy-fifth birthday, he jumped again, and from 12,500 feet landed on the lawn at his Presidential Library in College Station, Texas.

Before the jump he'd assured Mrs. Bush it would be his last jump, but she knew better, predicting he'd jump five years later to celebrate his eightieth birthday, which of course he did, again, at his Presidential Library, in 2004. The former president leapt from a plane flying 120 miles per hour at thirteen thousand feet. He even jumped a second time just after tandem jumps by Fox News anchor Brit Hume and martial arts movie star Chuck Norris. Former Soviet premier Mikhail Gorbachev declined an invitation to jump, quipping, "Maybe on his ninetieth birthday."

President Bush's 2007 jump, though, at age eighty-three and having just recovered from a hip replacement, was a masterful "sneak attack." After renovations and remodeling, his Presidential Library, which had initially been unveiled ten years earlier, held a grand re-opening ceremony outside the museum. Jim Nantz served as emcee and directed the crowd to look skyward to see the "Golden Knights Parachute Demonstration."

After the Knights had all jumped out of their aircraft, guess who jumped out next?

President Bush, in tandem with Sergeant Major Elliott!

Nantz revealed the identity of the last jumper to the delight and surprise of the crowd, which included his children Governor Jeb Bush and daughter Doro.

After he landed and eventually took the podium, President Bush said simply, "You've got to do things that are fun. I don't have to sit around drooling because I'm eighty-three."

He then admitted the Golden Knights team made him feel like he was twenty-three.

When the president turned eighty-five in June of 2009, he decided to skydive over good ol' Kennebunkport.

The plan for the jump was that the president would jump from 10,500 feet and touch down on a small piece of land along the sea in the St. Ann's Church yard.

"George, why would you choose to land on that little spot?" Bar asked him before the jump.

"Well, if something goes wrong they won't have to move the body very far. Just drag me right over to the church," he joked.

Robin Meade, a reporter from CNN's Headline News, jumped with him. President Bush tried to get Nantz to jump with him too, but Nantz declined. His contract at CBS likely did not allow for him to engage in dangerous activities such as skydiving.

Once again the free fall was with Sergeant Elliott, who guided the two of them to a landing on the oceanfront lawn of St. Ann's, just down Ocean Drive from Walker's Point.

After President Bush landed safely at St. Ann's, some of the Bushes' grandchildren took the opportunity to skydive with the Golden Knights throughout the weekend.

At age ninety, President Bush was not to be denied, despite some real health scares in the years since his last skydive. He jumped tandem again with Sergeant Elliott over Kennebunkport in June of 2014, but this time they jumped out of a helicopter because it was more stable for President Bush than an airplane. The key ingredient was he had to be able to hold his legs straight out at the landing, even with his legs largely immobilized by the Parkinson's disease that keeps him confined to a wheelchair. Elliott wore a Go-Pro camera on his helmet throughout the jump, and on television the president could be seen in a helmet and goggles.

Many of the Bushes' dear friends, family members, locals and extended family stood, as we did, on the grass along the Atlantic Ocean with both Mrs. Bush and former President George W. Bush, along with his daughters Jenna and Barbara, peering skyward looking for the "birthday boy," who, in 1944, had parachuted into the Pacific.

A red, white, and blue canopy opened and circled above the land. Eventually Elliott, with President Bush sliding on his knees in front of him, swept down and skidded to a stop, face down, on the lawn, drawing gasps from the gathered crowd. If he was hurt, though, he sure wasn't going to let anyone know it.

Grandchildren Barbara and Jenna Bush approached singing "Happy Birthday" to their "Gampy" as he was placed in his wheelchair, and someone in the crowd yelled out "We love you, Mr. President!"

#43 gave his father a hug and said, "Good jump."

His father answered, "It was nice."

"How'd you feel?"

"Cold," came his answer.

It was early June in Maine, after all.

Mrs. Bush, in a turtleneck with a pink quilted vest, approached her husband and said, "Not bad. Are you all right?"

"Yep," said the president.

"Did they have to push you out?" she joked.

"No," he answered. "I got confused. They did all the work."

Mrs. Bush then gave him a touching, loving kiss.

The largely self-effacing Bush Family still follows the philosophy set by Dorothy Bush: "Nobody likes a braggadocio."

That night a special ninetieth birthday party took place at Hidden Pond, a sixty-acre resort of luxury cottages in a birch forest on Goose Rocks Road in Kennebunkport. There were lots of toasts and following dinner, the "Irish Tenor" Ronan Tynan serenaded the crowd of about 150 people, all of whom had either seen the jump in person or on national television.

President Bush has stated many times that one of the greatest honors he has ever had was having an aircraft carrier named after him. It is a Nimitz-class supercarrier completed in 2009 at a cost of $6.2 billion.

Anne and I, along with many friends, attended the commissioning of the SS *George H. W. Bush* (CVN-77) in Norfolk, Virginia. It was an incredible experience. There were about fifteen thousand people there and we were lucky enough to have seats on the dock for the commissioning as the command was transferred to the captain. Doro Bush Koch, the president's daughter, who was sponsor of the ship, gave the ceremonial order to "man our ship and bring her to life!" What seemed like thousands of crewmembers filed on board, up and down the gangplanks in their whites. When they reached the top deck, they stood at attention all around the perimeter of the aircraft carrier. We sat with a large group from the Kennebunks as the president spoke from the deck of the aircraft carrier. Some of the shipbuilders spoke, and the ship was then placed at the command of Rear Admiral Nora Tyson.

Back in Maine, we also had thought a lot about how we might honor President Bush. Here we had a president of the United States who lives in Kennebunkport and cherishes the town. It would simply be wrong if we didn't somehow acknowledge that as citizens of the town. Nancy Sosa, a very charitable, active local resident, Tom Bradbury, who runs the Conservation Trust in Kennebunkport, and I got a small committee together, and we began to wonder what could we do to salute the man we loved. We wanted to create something that other people could enjoy and commemorate the fact that President Bush lived there.

I'm a guy who works at a golf club that was founded in 1896, so I often think about the traditions of the past and our responsibilities for the future. One hundred years from now, when we're all gone, would we have done our part to share the portion of history in which we lived? We need to document some of these things, so we did some research.

We finally came up with the idea of marking the president's presence with a large anchor as a monument. It seemed like an appropriate symbol since he was a naval officer who lived on the ocean and loved boating and the sea. We set out trying to figure out how to get an anchor and started a quiet fundraising campaign to pay for the anchor and its granite stone base and create a plaque to go with it. Bradbury and the Conservation Trust secured a small piece of land on Ocean Avenue at Blowing Rock Cove over-looking Walker's Point. It was a perfect location because thousands of people pulled their cars over and stopped there in the summer to take photos of the president's home on Walker's Point across the cove. Now they'd have something else to enhance the experience — a giant anchor and a plaque.

We knew that we could raise the funds (enough to maintain the anchor for years), but where would we even find something like a giant anchor?

I serve as golf professional at Coral Creek Club, near Boca Grande, Florida, in the winter. One of our members brought Sean O'Keefe to the club as his guest. I happened to remember he was the former secretary of the navy, and we were having trouble finding an anchor, so I approached him on the subject of procuring one.

"It's a great idea," he told me. "I'd be happy to support the project and help you try to get one."

O'Keefe meant what he said, because the next thing we knew he ended up presenting choices of four anchors! We picked out a three-ton, very large anchor from a military destroyer ship from the mid-Atlantic coast area. We had it refinished and shipped up to Kennebunkport.

We secretly worked with President Bush's staff and his speechwriter Jim McGrath on how the bronze plaque accompanying the anchor would read. We discreetly cleared the little piece of land and put in some flowers to make the spot presentable. The Secret Service was in on our plan, too, so, for a while, whenever they drove the president somewhere during the day they turned right out of the house instead of left, no matter where they were going, to stop #41 from noticing any activity around the area.

After checking with the Kennebunkport Police and city officials, we arranged to have Ocean Avenue closed at 10:00 a.m. on September 30, 2009, in order to stage a surprise ceremony for the president and unveil the anchor. We set up folding chairs on the road facing the anchor, which was covered with a tarp. The tarp was decorated with painted handprints of local art students in Janet Wendle's class at Consolidated School. A podium with a microphone was set up and I was honored to serve as master of ceremonies.

It was Barbara Bush's responsibility to get her husband to the surprise ceremony without him knowing about it ahead of time.

"George," she told him that morning, "Kenny Raynor called from the club. He asked if you wouldn't mind coming up to the golf course. He wants to see you at ten o'clock."

"Okay," he shrugged. "Do you know what he wanted?"

"No, I'm not sure," she answered. "He just said he'd appreciate it if you came up there."

She sold her bill of goods really well using my name. Because I never had, nor would I ever, summon the president to the golf course like that!

At 10:00 a.m. President Bush got in the car to be driven "to the golf course." The car this time turned left out of the gate, went about 150 yards, and stopped because Ocean Avenue was closed. When he had to get out of the car, it became apparent very quickly that something was going on. A brass band and a bagpiper filled the air with music. He took a seat and I introduced Sosa and Bradbury, who both spoke, and the Bushes' granddaughter Lauren Bush, to represent the family spoke about her "Gampy."

Bob Paine, a local artist, presented the Bushes with a painting of the scene, and museum director Tracy Baetz presented a card signed by hundreds of visitors.

Finally the anchor was unveiled, to the delight of the Bushes and the applause from the crowd. The plaque read: ANCHOR TO WINDWARD. FOR OUR FRIEND AND 41ST PRESIDENT GEORGE H. W. BUSH. AS HE WAS FOR OUR NATION AND WORLD DURING FOUR YEARS OF TUMULTUOUS AND HISTORIC CHANGE, SO, TOO HAS KENNEBUNKPORT SERVED, IN THE WORDS OF ST. PAUL, "AS AN ANCHOR OF THE SOUL, BOTH SURE AND STEAD" TO HIM. PRESENTED BY THOSE WHO LOVE HIM AS MUCH AS HE LOVES THIS SPECIAL PLACE.

The president was humbled and, as he spoke at the microphone, with the giant anchor, the cove, and his house on Walker's Point behind him, he became overwhelmed with gratitude and invited everyone to come over to Walker's Point to "see the anchor from the other point of view."

This spontaneous invitation was to Bar's dismay. She had a normal day ahead when she woke up that morning. Suddenly she's at a 10:00 a.m. dedication ceremony across the cove. Next thing she knows, without warning, she has 150 people walking down the sidewalk and turning toward the gate headed for her house!

"I knew he was going to do that," is all Mrs. Bush said.

That day, we realized something needed to be done to honor Barbara Bush, as well. The same committee put its heads together and realized that since Mrs. Bush loved her gardening, it would be a nice thing if the Conservation Trust might find a piece of land to create a garden as a tribute to Bar. The Conservancy did, indeed, have a lovely spot right on the Village Green in front of the Captain Lord Mansion across from Arundel Yacht Club and within blocks of Dock Square—the center of Kennebunkport.

Since all of her grandchildren call her "Ganny," it was obvious we should name it "Ganny's Garden." And again, as we had for the anchor site, in secret, we created the garden. The grandkids' initials are engraved in random spots on the garden's small stone walls, which surround colorful flower beds and planted trees around the garden. A stone pathway winds through and leads to a commemorative plaque and a bench upon which a bronzed, straw sun hat—the type Mrs. Bush is known to wear—sits near a bronzed copy of her favorite book, *Pride and Prejudice* (also a nod to her efforts to promote literacy), left as if she'd just been there.

If she had been, Mrs. Bush would have left her shoes, because you can see a pair of her mismatched Keds sneakers next to the bench, too. She likes to wear two different-colored Keds at one time. It's become her fun trademark, but surely it is difficult for her to match them up since she may, by now, have been given more pairs than Imelda Marcos!

On the September 2011 morning of what was again to be a surprise dedication, Bar went off with her aide to get her hair done. On the way back from the hair salon, she could not proceed because Ocean Avenue had been blocked off with a tent on the Village Green. The president loved it because now he got to surprise Bar after she'd been in on surprising him for the anchor dedication a couple of years earlier.

Bar got out of the car and wondered what was going on. Quickly she was escorted to her seat for the ceremony. Like her husband had been, she was clearly startled and moved. She was also playfully mad at her personal aide for not clueing her in that this was happening so she could have her customary four strings of pearls and proper attire on. She was concerned she was dressed inappropriately. Of course nobody cared at all—they just loved her so much and were thrilled to be part of the ceremony. Nevertheless, her friend and Kennebunkport neighbor Alicia Spenlinhauer gave Bar her necklace to wear.

The Keds company sent the former first lady even more sneakers, which were presented to her in the ceremony under the tent at the garden attended by the former president, US senator Susan Collins, and Maine governor Paul LePage's wife Ann (Maine's First Lady).

As festive as the day was, Mrs. Bush, when she rose to speak, couldn't help but recall an emotional spring day in 1993.

"When we first came back after George lost the election, you had a ceremony on this lawn and you made us feel that it was OK to lose and that we were among friends," she said. "George Bush and I feel at home here."

The plaque in the garden reads:

IN HONOR OF BARBARA PIERCE BUSH

FIRST LADY OF THE UNITED STATES

FAMILY LITERACY ADVOCATE

DEVOTED WIFE, MOTHER, GRANDMOTHER, FRIEND

VOLUNTEER AND PHILANTHROPIC WORK IS A LOT LIKE PLANTING PEONIES,

YOU MAY NOT SEE THE RESULTS RIGHT AWAY

BUT YOU ARE PLANTING SEEDS WHICH WILL ONE DAY SPROUT AND BLOOM FOREVER.

— BARBARA BUSH

DEDICATED BY THOSE WHO ADMIRE THIS SINGULAR WOMAN AND HER COUNTLESS CONTRIBUTIONS TO OUR WORLD.

9

TURKEY DAY DURING LAME DUCK

It was springtime 1993, and the eastern seaboard village of Kennebunkport, Maine was coming alive with new growth: plants and flowers were blooming in the warm sea air with a bright blue sky overhead. Another new career was blossoming, too: private life for George and Barbara Bush in Kennebunkport.

Hundreds gathered on the Village Green for a rally to welcome the now former president and Mrs. Bush back to Kennebunkport for the first time as private citizens since leaving the Oval Office. Following President Clinton's inauguration in January, they'd wintered in Houston and had just arrived back at Walker's Point for the summer, as they do each May.

Kennebunkport's Village Green is across from the Arundel Yacht Club, virtually on the lawn of the Captain Lord Mansion Bed and Breakfast.

The town turned out that day in order to show their affection and give their "George and Barbara" a collective "welcome home." There was a high school band, some fire trucks, and some speeches made and gifts given.

One of the things I did for President Bush, as a joke during the welcome home ceremony, was to present him with one of the extra-long putters—one that he made famous during his presidential years when he played golf—but with a twist: The contraption had a fly-reel on one end and a putter-head on the other with some feathers hanging off of it. The sentiment was that I hoped the president would sit back and enjoy his life and partake in the activities he loves with family and friends.

It was all smiles and laughs that spring afternoon—and "CAVU" as the president liked to optimistically describe life's situations and opportunities. "CAVU" was "pilot code" to describe weather conditions: "Ceiling And Visibility Unlimited."

But six months earlier the sky had been as dark as everyone's mood. On Thanksgiving weekend of 1992, the president and Mrs. Bush had come to Kennebunkport after losing the 1992 election, which was emotional for all of us. It was a cold November. The skies were gray. The trees had lost all their leaves.

About a week or two before the election, I played golf at Cape Arundel with Gen. Brent Scowcroft. General Scowcroft has a home in Kennebunkport and is a member at Cape Arundel. From time to time I would give him golf lessons or we'd go out and play six holes or whatever he had time for. We might hit shots, and sometimes we just sat in the cart and talked. We talked about what was going on in their world. Every time we spoke it was evident General Scowcroft had huge respect for President Bush. It wasn't all politics.

During this particular round, though, we talked about our concerns regarding the election.

We walked off the seventh green and put our putters back into each of our golf bags and sat down in the cart. Before I drove to the next tee, I looked at Scowcroft and stated the obvious in the form of a question. "Governor Clinton puts on quite a presentation, doesn't he?"

"He sure does. Ross Perot does, too, in his own way," he answered. "But Kenny, when you're campaigning for president, or any office, you have to be willing, even eager, to talk about yourself. You and I both know that's not what George Bush is all about. The subject he least likes to talk about is himself."

General Scowcroft was right. George Bush wants to talk about you. If you ever meet him, you'll understand. You'll be in awe about meeting a president and the next thing you know you'll be talking about yourself and he'll be the one listening. Not vice versa.

"How are you doing? Where are you from? How long have you been playing golf?" He's an instant question guy, not an instant answer guy.

There were times when we'd be coming off the golf course and members of the press would yell out, "How did it go, Mr. President? How did you play?"

I knew he didn't want to answer and talk about himself, so I'd answer for him and try to shine the light on him: "The president played great today. He had two birdies!"

In turn he would happily tell them about me: "My pro here shot 68!"

He would always deflect the subject so it was never about him.

It's hard to get elected under those circumstances.

We had our concerns.

Our hearts sank as Anne and I watched the election returns, and President Bush's concession speech from the Westin Galleria Hotel in Houston, on television. He took to the podium looking pained but speaking with authority.

"Here's the way we see it and the country should see it. The people have spoken. We respect the majesty of the democratic system," he insisted. "I just called Governor Clinton in Little Rock and offered my congratulations. He did run a strong campaign. I wish him well in the White House."

And then, in George Bush fashion, he began to help the president-elect.

"And I want the country to know that our entire administration will work closely with his team. There is important work to do, and America must always come first. So we will get behind this new president and wish him well."

The president wore a dark, lightly pinstriped suit with a slate blue tie, and, while their children and grandchildren stood behind them, Mrs. Bush, in front of red, white, and blue balloons, wearing a red dress with white pearls, smiled with admiration at her husband as he even thanked his campaign directors, saying they "ran a valiant effort in a very, very, difficult year."

After thanking General Scowcroft and taking a sip of water, the president said, "Of course I want to thank my family, with a special emphasis on a woman named 'Barbara.'" The crowd roared with applause. "She's inspired this entire nation and I think the country will always be grateful."

She was the picture of dignity, as was the president, who continued, "As for me I am going to serve and try to find ways to help people, but I am going to get very active in the 'grandchild business.'"

It was a sweet sentiment and we were excited for the time he'd have with his family, but we were filled with great disappointment for him as well. Anne and I were upset for our country and for the world, too, because we knew how well he was perceived and what his accomplishments were concerning the end of the Cold War, the fall of the Berlin Wall, and the liberation of Kuwait from the tyranny of Iraqi dictator Saddam Hussein. President George H. W. Bush was an international hero and to see him rejected by the voters here in America was surprising if not startling.

There was one member of his family President Bush would not have much more time to spend with, though. In an unbelievably cruel twist of fate, two weeks after the election loss, his mother, Dorothy Walker Bush, died of a stroke in her home in Connecticut. The president had flown from Washington to see her and arrived back only hours before her passing. The funeral service for the ninety-one-year-old matriarch was in Greenwich.

Dorothy Walker was born in Kennebunkport in 1901. It was her father, George Herbert Walker, a banker, who, in 1922, founded golf's long-running Walker Cup Match, which pits a team of American amateur players against a squad of amateurs from Great Britain and Ireland. Walker was also president of the United States Golf Association at the time. The first formal match was held at National Golf Links in New York, and, like the subsequent Ryder Cup matches staged for professionals, the US team was dominant over the years and leads the now biennial series 35–9 as of 2015.

The Walker Cup venues in England, Ireland, Scotland, and Wales have been at classic courses including the Old Course at St. Andrews, Turnberry, Royal Birkdale, Muirfield, Royal St. George's, Portmarnock, Royal Liverpool, Sunningdale, Royal Porthcawl, Nairn, Ganton, Royal County Down, Royal Aberdeen, Royal Lytham, and St. Anne's—each of which, by the way, is available for unaccompanied guest play.

On the US side of the pond, the Walker Cup Match has been staged at largely exclusive enclaves including Garden City Golf Club, Chicago Golf Club, The Country Club (near Boston), Pine Valley, in New Jersey (which trades places with Northern Ireland's Royal County Down at the top of the list of "Golf Magazine World Top 100 Courses"), Winged Foot, Kittansett, the Minikahda Club, Seattle Golf Club, Baltimore County Club, Milwaukee Country Club, Shinnecock, Cypress Point, Peachtree, Interlachen, Quaker Ridge, Ocean Forest, Merion, and Los Angeles Country Club.

Dorothy Walker, in 1921, married Prescott Bush, also a banker who would go on to become USGA president—in addition to being elected to the US Senate. They were married at the Church of St. Ann in Kennebunkport, just down along the ocean from the family summer home on Walker's Point. It's doubtful that Dorothy and Prescott, on their wedding day, could ever have imagined that, ninety-three years later on June 12, their son, having survived being shot down and forced to bail from an Avenger bomber over the Pacific Ocean off the coast of Japan in the Second World War, would purposely parachute into that same grassy churchyard to celebrate his ninetieth birthday!

A free fall is what many would have thought Bush's world seemed to be in that autumn. But President Bush, by all accounts, did his best to conceal personal disappointment during that November of 1992, when he lost his reelection bid and his beloved mother. He even gamely smiled through one of the silliest annual White House traditions, the "Thanksgiving Turkey Pardon," after becoming a "lame duck" president. During the ceremony President

Bush posed with a turkey and assured the elementary school children that, due to the pardon he issued, the turkey's fate would be to live out the rest of its years at a Virginia farm.

"Take it easy, turkey, we're just here to serve you," he joked to the bird.

The president then said, "This is a time to remember all the good things we've been given and ask ourselves what good we can find to do."

That is the question that may have been on George H. W. Bush's mind when he and the first lady left Washington, DC to come to Kennebunkport for Thanksgiving.

The media seemed intent on painting the first couple's visit to Kennebunkport as a thankless retreat. After all, Maine voters had voted for Clinton, then Perot . . . then Bush.

Thanksgiving is definitely a "shoulder season" in Kennebunkport, Maine. The summer tourists are long gone. "Leaf season" is over, and the "Currier and Ives" frosting of snow has yet to fall, so the place is colorless. A number of the more popular restaurants, like Mabel's Lobster Claw, have shuttered for the season, and the Christmas season Prelude festival, which bathes Dock Square in lights and hails Santa Claus's arrival on a lobster boat, is still weeks away.

But it wasn't really a surprise to me that the president would want to make his way to Kennebunkport after a disappointing defeat. After all, his Walker's Point home is his self-described "anchor to windward." There he could take power walks on Parson's Beach and view the beautiful scenery. He'd stay active for the weekend and soothe his disappointment by going back to a place he loves.

We had just closed the golf course for the season, so the tee markers had been taken in and the flagsticks were out of the greens. But just after dawn, on a damp, cold morning, I got a phone call at home. It was the president himself.

"Kenny, is the golf course still open and ready for play?"

"Uh, well . . . "

"Can we play at nine o'clock?" he asked.

The course wasn't open, and it wasn't scheduled to be ready for play until May.

"Yes, Mr. President," I answered, of course. "The weather should be okay. I will see you at nine o'clock. Let's tee it up!"

We hung up, and I knew, with no tee markers set and no flagsticks in the ground, I had about seventy-five minutes to get over to Cape Arundel and get the course ready. I called our superintendent and phoned Bill, my wife's brother, in a desperate attempt to get another body out there so we could get the flagsticks back in and put tee markers out in time! We went charging over to the golf course and, like manic worker bees, tried to beat the clock. We covered all eighteen holes of the golf course, planting flagsticks, tee markers, and cleaning carts to get ready for the presidential entourage. Then it was time for me to quickly switch hats and get ready to hit an opening tee shot!

The presidential limousine and motorcade pulled in just before nine o'clock and I hustled out to the parking lot, still out of breath, to greet him. He emerged from the limousine and shook my hand.

"Good morning, Mr. President. Glad you could make it. It's a beautiful day for autumn golf," I said, tongue in cheek.

The first thing he said, with a twinkle in his eye, was, "Kenny . . . you've been busy, haven't you? There weren't any flagsticks in when we drove by the course on our way in last night!"

We all laughed out loud at his little trick and then went off to play the freshly "reopened" course.

Did we talk about the election loss? I simply acknowledged it briefly as a friend would about any disappointment. We certainly didn't dwell on the loss, because the golf course and our friendship existed as an oasis of escape for activity and fun.

Did he seem down? How could he not have been.

The resulting *New York Times* headline read: IN MAINE, PRESIDENT AND WIFE SPEND PRIVATE THANKSGIVING, and the story of the round, with the byline "Special to the *New York Times*," detailed what had happened, but without any of the playfulness. It read: "Despite a steady drizzle and a temperature in the 40's, Mr. Bush played two hours of golf on a soggy Cape Arundel course near his home with Ken Raynor, the club's professional."

In a change from past procedure, reporters were not allowed onto the course, although they could watch from the road. Mr. Bush, who would sometimes chat with reporters at the clubhouse, "[wanted] his privacy and we're facilitating that," a White House press aide said.

There was no media, though, for George H. W. Bush's last official round of golf at Cape Arundel as the 41st president of the United States. It was played on November 29—the last day of his post-election Thanksgiving visit before he would return to Washington to wrap up his presidency. Between those responsibilities, the weather, and his travel schedule, he'd not be in a position to play golf again until after the inauguration of President-Elect Bill Clinton.

Without the press, and because the club was closed for the season, it was a quiet round at Cape Arundel. Thankfully, White House photographer David Valdez unobtrusively documented some of the significant moments.

The eighteenth hole at Cape Arundel is a par-4 playing uphill often into the prevailing wind. The clubhouse—now known as "41 House" in the president's honor—is on the left side about halfway down the hole that plays over the club's driveway in from River Road. The tee sits at the edge of the Kennebunk River, which the tee shots must carry to reach the fairway safely.

When we reached the eighteenth tee, we realized this would be President Bush's last drive as commander-in-chief at Cape Arundel—the last time the playfully self-described "Mr. Smooth" would smooth a shot down the fairway. As head golf professional, I suggested David Valdez be certain to capture the moment for posterity with a photo.

"Oh it's so melodramatic. Let's lighten it up a bit and make it fun," Mrs. Bush suggested. "Why don't we all hit our drives at the same time?"

"You bet, Bar! It's the last drive of the 'Silver Fox' as first lady, too!" said the president. "Pro, mine, c'mon in the middle between us there. Let's let 'em fly!"

With the first lady on my left and the president on my right, we counted out loud to three and struck simultaneous drives.

As we got closer to the green, I could see that Anne had brought our two-year-old son Kyle out to greet us when we came off the golf course. Before we finished the hole, we waved them up to the eighteenth green. Little Kyle came trundling out in boots, white sweatpants, and a fleece.

There was just enough autumn sun to cast a shadow. George Herbert Walker Bush, as he had so many times over the decades on this very green, stood over the last putt of the round. This time, though, the six-foot putt would be his last as president of the United States.

"Big Guy, can you hold the flagstick for this one? Can you take it from your father?" the president said to Kyle, with a smile. Of course the significance was lost on Kyle, but he loved helping, and still does to this day. I handed him the flagstick, which was at least three times as tall as him and flapping in the wind. He put his little hands around the metal and held on tight.

And with that, President Bush drew back his putter and let it roll.

Did that particular putt fall?

It doesn't really matter.

The clubhouse was deserted and the air had grown colder, so there wasn't a lot of dawdling. We waved goodbye as the first couple pulled away. At the time I thought it would be the last time I would ever be with a sitting US president (which, due to George W. being elected president, proved to be wrong). But more to the point, I knew my friend would have a lot of miles on him by the next time I saw him. And I figured Kennebunkport would be a lot brighter, more colorful, and warmer by the time I did.

On Monday I got a phone call from Ed Flynn, the resident Secret Service agent at Walker's Point.

"Ken, when you get a chance can you come down to the house? I've got something for you," he said.

Later in the day I drove over, and through the security gate, to meet him at his command post, which is to the right after the guardhouse.

"President Bush was at the helicopter pad here and about to leave Walker's Point aboard *Marine One* for the last time as president," said Flynn. "He was about to step aboard the chopper but he suddenly said, 'Hold on, I forgot something,' and went back into the house."

I listened with interest.

"He came back out with this box and asked me to remember to give it to you."

I opened the box to find an eight-by-ten photo of President Bush in a stainless steel frame etched with the presidential seal. In the photo he was smiling broadly and leaning on a golf club while wearing a red cap and a red, white, and blue jacket. There was a handwritten message in the bottom border.

"As I leave Kennebunkport for the last time as president, I send you my thanks, my profound thanks, for your many courtesies . . . but the best is yet to come. God Speed, George Bush."

Today I still feel the tears and emotions of that moment!

Paul Marchand, Director of Golf at The Summit Club, Celebrity Golf Coach, and Past President's Cup Vice-Captain

I was the pro at Houston Country Club when President Bush and Barbara came back to town after his re-election defeat in 1992. It was definitely a challenging time for the president. Getting to know him better now, and looking back on it, as a competitor I know he was extremely disappointed to not have a second term.

The Bushes had previously been longtime members of the great, old Houston Country Club before his years serving in Washington, DC. When the president rejoined, it was his intention to be a "real" member, so he would go around and personally introduce himself to the staff and thank them for making lunch. That's the kind of guy he is.

He came into the golf shop looking for me and sat down at my office desk. In a short amount of time we found we had a lot in common in terms of values. Miraculously we became very good friends. To their credit, the Bushes like having friends in their lives who are not important, influential people. They just like others and they enjoy people and like being connected in a kind and friendly way.

10
GLORY'S LAST SHOT

The president has been an incredibly active man throughout his life. When he was vice president and then as president and now former president, a normal vacation day started with a little office time first thing in the morning at about 6:00 a.m. Then he might go out fishing, or get some exercise by taking a power walk, or play a few sets of tennis. After lunch a round of golf might be in order. He'd have guests in for dinner, or go out, and then be early to bed by nine o'clock. In between all that was working time. He's done all that as long as I have known him. You might call him a man who loves all that life has to offer.

Mark Plummer, 13-Time Maine State Amateur Champion

I was playing on a Sunday morning at 6:00 a.m. with President Bush #41, President Bush #43, and golf pro Kenny Raynor. The presidents had to meet their first ladies Barbara and Laura at church at 9:00 a.m., hence the early tee time.

At one point I picked up President Bush's ball on the green and marked it for him. When I looked at it, I saw it was a Titleist 41 with the presidential seal on it. Also printed on the ball were the letters "FLFW."

I handed the ball to President Bush.

"Sir," I asked him, "I realize the '41' is printed on the ball because you were the 41st president, but what do the letters FLFW on your ball stand for?"

He answered simply, "Former leader of the free world."

I should have known!

Having had a few cups of coffee on my ninety-minute ride down to Cape Arundel Golf Club, by the time we reached the seventh hole, Mother Nature was calling. I spotted some bushes (no pun intended) on the right-hand side of the fairway. While I was relieving myself I noticed two Secret Service men carrying rifles standing right beside me! Upon returning to the fairway, I told the 41st president of my encounter, and told him I'd never felt so safe taking a leak. We had a big laugh.

My rounds with President Bush have created some of the fondest memories of my life. The experiences were almost surreal. To have the honor of playing golf with the president, and getting to know him and his wonderful family, is something I never would have even dreamed of. I dearly miss our rounds of golf together, but continue to enjoy seeing him a couple of times each summer. He and Barbara are truly amazing people. Their friendship with me and my wife Alison is something I cherish deeply.

In the Spring of 2007, days before President Bush's eighty-third birthday, during one of our many rounds, he brought up a challenge involving golf.

"Kenny, is it okay if I come to the range and hit some balls with you?"

"Of course, Mr. President," I answered, using the inflection of a question.

"You know that I am allergic to practice, right?"

"I do, sir," I answered.

"Just hearing the word 'practice' makes me break out into hives."

"Yes, sir."

"But Tiger Woods contacted my office. He's invited me to come to Congressional Country Club near Washington for the PGA Tour he's hosting to benefit the US Troops . . ."

I listened, nodding, knowing an appearance by the president would be great for the troops and for the game of golf.

"And Tiger wants me to hit the ceremonial opening tee shot."

Because it was for the troops, and because it was Tiger asking, the president told Woods he would do it. He had met Woods at the Ryder Cup and President's Cup Matches, and Tiger had given him a spontaneous lesson on sand play in a bunker at Jack Nicklaus's Muirfield Village Golf Club in Columbus, Ohio. Woods had placed tees all over the practice green and was hitting shots from the bunker to the tiny tee locations. It didn't matter where on the green the tees were, Tiger could hit shots right to them from the sand. President Bush came back to Kennebunkport and stopped by the golf shop at Cape Arundel after that trip with a gray, Muirfield Village member's blazer with the club logo on the breast.

"Yeah I was hanging around hitting shots with Tiger Woods this weekend," he said jokingly. "I'm a 'name dropper.' You would not believe his skill and talent. It seemed like every shot he hit landed four inches from the target!"

President Bush never looked at it like he was the star. It was Nicklaus and Woods who should be "name dropping" that they hit balls with George Bush.

I knew this opening tee shot, which would be on the Fourth of July, was going to be a spectacle. I knew the former commander-in-chief would be asked to step up to the tee surrounded by soldiers, sailors, airmen, and marines, plus the media cameras, and, with the world's number-one golfer, plus a crowd of who knows how many in the gallery, and hit an inspiring tee shot. I knew George H. W. Bush would want to deliver. He needed to deliver! And it would likely be the last time he would play golf in public under such celebrated circumstances.

"Perfect. Let's go. You'll do great," I told him, thrilled for my dear friend.

President Bush and I spent thirty days of practice preparing him to hit this single, ceremonial opening drive. Those were very special sessions of quality time each day practicing alone together. His Suburban would pull into the parking lot, we'd go out behind the clubhouse, and he'd hit balls across the tenth and eighteenth fairways down toward the seventh tee for fifteen or twenty minutes, or sometimes half an hour. He'd just hit drivers trying to work out his golf swing and give him the confidence he needed. He always could hit drives, but, in the case of this ceremonial tee shot, he would only have one try.

In terms of equipment for this patriotic endeavor, I ordered a 13.5-degree McGregor driver to help President Bush launch the ball up in the air. Playing with loft, particularly when all he had to do was hit one drive well, would be helpful for the president since his normal ball-flight was a slight cut to the right or a top. Together we set up the ceremonial driver with loft and a lighter, softer shaft to provide success.

I went to see the president the morning of the ceremonial tee shot before he flew down to Washington.

He looked at me and said, "You know, Ken, I spoke in front of a million people in Poland at the end of the Cold War. I wasn't nervous one bit. Today, I am scared to death of hitting this tee shot."

"That's the game of golf for you, isn't it, Mr. President?"

Off he went to execute the mission: the nerve-wracking tee shot that had been driving him crazy for a month.

From what the president told me the next day upon his return to Kennebunkport, and from what I saw on national television and the evening newscast, it had been a spectacle, all right. There were military bands and a flyover and a big crowd of uniformed servicemen and women.

President Bush told me that when he arrived at the course Woods met him with a big smile and lots of appreciation for his participation.

"Mr. President, would you like to go hit some balls and warm up some before we bring you out in front of the crowd? It's a sold-out house for you!"

He did, and so they went quietly to the practice range where Woods would watch him warm up.

"Kenny, I topped the very first practice ball I tried to hit. Then I shanked the second one. I snap-hooked the third one; and I dribbled the fourth one right in front of me."

Then he turned to Tiger and pronounced, "Okay, I'm ready. Let's go."

The president could tell that Woods was horrified at seeing those four dreadful shots. Woods had presumed he was a better golfer than that and was fearful the grand opening of his tournament was not going to go as he thought it would go.

At the tee, when introduced, President Bush, wearing khakis, a red golf shirt with thin horizontal stripes, and a white cap, received a standing ovation. He smiled, waved, and then got to the business of taking dead aim. With PGA Tour commissioner Tim Finchem, the crowd, and the television audience watching, and Woods holding his breath, Bush drew the driver back, just as he'd practiced . . . and powered a drive down the middle of the fairway about 220 yards, with a touch of draw on it for good measure! The crowd cheered and Woods broke into one of those patented, priceless Tiger grins.

That drive was a look into the competitive soul of #41. He does what it takes and did what it took.

I knew deep down that the golf shot would work out though, because I'd seen him do it before — also under pressure.

President Bush, in 1990, accepted Honorary Membership in the Royal and Ancient Golf Club at St. Andrews, Scotland — the birthplace of golf. The club, golf's ruling body, in bestowing the membership, cited the president's long connection with the sport. President Bush's grandfather, Herbert Walker, was a USGA president who donated the Walker Cup for matches contested every two years between a team of amateur golfers from America and a squad from Great Britain/Ireland. The president's father, US senator Prescott Bush, was also a USGA president.

To distinguish that honor, the president made himself available to travel to St. Andrews to attend the members' Fall Meeting and play in the member "three ball" tournament they hold with the annual changing of the captains. It's a big ceremonial deal for which a large crowd gathers along the Old Course's first tee, which is right in the corner of town, to watch the outgoing captain hit a tee shot. The church bells then chime and the incoming captain, while a cannon on the tee fires, hits his tee shot, which sets off a mad flurry down the fairway because whichever caddie gets to the incoming captain's tee ball first returns it to the new captain where the captain, by centuries-old tradition, buys the ball back with a gold sovereign coin.

President Bush was playing in the group with the incoming captain, Gordon Jeffrey, so after all of that pomp and circumstance, he then had to hit a tee shot in front of a giant crowd at the home of golf. The outgoing captain, Lord Griffiths, and Jeffrey were nearly scratch golfers who played basically to the quality of touring pros and had both cracked beautiful drives. President Bush had to follow them, and he was very nervous. He was taking practice swings on the tee to stay loose until one of the caddies interrupted him. "Sir," the caddie advised the president, "in Scotland we don't take practice swings on the tee. Would you please step off the tee and take practice swings adjacent to it?"

I stood at the rail and watched with great interest as the president struck the best drive I have ever seen him hit in all my years. He striped it solid right down the center, to the approval of the crowd, just as well as the captains had! It was a proud moment for me, as his golf professional, and a great moment for American golf in general. I walked the outgoing nine on the Old Course with him and he played beautifully, carding 39 at the turn.

Bobby Wilson, Five-Time World Long Drive Champion and Long Drive Hall of Famer

I had the opportunity to play golf with President George H. W. Bush at Mauna Lani Resort on the Big Island of Hawaii in 1998. Pepsi-Co was celebrating their one hundredth anniversary and they brought him in for a couple of days to speak.

One of his staff members told me he likes to have someone to play golf with.

"Would you mind playing with him?" I was asked.

It was one of the greatest things I have ever had the opportunity to do!

There were a couple of Secret Service agents around, but mostly it was like playing with your grandfather and listening to him tell stories. It was magnificent.

President Bush talked about how great it was to be on the golf course.

"It's an honor to be playing with you, Bobby," he actually told me. Of course it was quite the opposite.

I was enamored with him. He made me feel like I was his grandson.

Back at Cape Arundel one day, President Bush was at the club and seemed a little bit hesitant to talk to me about something—it turned out to be yet another honor he was receiving, with some golf involved.

"Kenny," he finally said, "I don't know if you're interested, but I'm going out to the World Series of Golf in Akron in a couple of weeks. They've decided to give me the Ambassador of Golf Award, and I wonder if you'd like to come with me? It won't be that exciting for you, though, because you can't play in the tournament—it's a PGA Tour pro-am."

"Sir, I understand that, but I'd be honored to come out with you and enjoy it."

"Well, they'll try to find somebody in the field who might want to play golf with me in the pro-am," he mused.

Of course he was being self-effacing because every PGA Tour player in that field would have loved to be the one partnered with President Bush.

"I'll play in the pro-am, accept the award that evening, and come back that night, so it's not an overnight trip," he explained.

"Mr. President, how about this," I suggested. "If you don't mind we'll team up and I will caddie for you?"

"Oh, no, Ken you don't want to caddie for me. They'll find someone who can carry the bag."

"Honestly, I think it would be fun. I know your game and I'll get to walk with you and we'll have some laughs out there."

"Really? Fine, then, if you're sure. That'd be great," he said.

We hopped an early morning private plane from Kennebunkport/Sanford Airport to Akron and were driven to Firestone Country Club, the longtime site of the World Series of Golf. It's a strange name for a golf tournament, and they don't call it that anymore, but it started as a made for television event pitting only the four Major Championship winners against each other. Eventually, and gradually, the field expanded.

When we arrived at Firestone, the organizers had a nice bungalow for us to use where we changed into our golf clothes and made our way out to the practice tee. Immediately most of the PGA Tour players stopped hitting practice balls to watch and some came over wanting to say hello to President Bush and shake his hand. Greg Norman, the Australian known as the "Great White Shark," because he'd loved to dive the Great Barrier Reef back home "down under," came over and gave him a big salute. Brad Faxon, a fellow New Englander, came over to say hello.

The event had assigned Hale Irwin as the president's pro-am foursome professional. Irwin, from Missouri, was a three-time US Open winner and won a number of other times on the PGA Tour, including three times at Hilton Head. He had high-profile wins at Pebble Beach in the Bing Crosby National Pro-Am and in the Los Angeles Open at Riviera Country Club. He won the very esteemed Western Open and Jack Nicklaus's Memorial Tournament, also in Ohio, at Muirfield Village near Columbus. Irwin was very cordial and subsequently visited Cape Arundel Golf Club with his son Steve.

There were thousands of spectators milling about the course that day, so when we arrived at the first tee it was lined with people. The president was very nervous, because the last thing he wanted to do was hit a wayward shot that might hit a spectator and injure someone.

"The last thing I want to do here is pull a 'Spiro Agnew' or a 'Gerald Ford,'" he joked.

In 1971, Vice President Agnew, playing in the Bob Hope Desert Classic in Palm Springs, was in a foursome with Hope, baseball star Willie Mays, and PGA Tour player Doug Sanders, whom Agnew had hit in the head with a wayward golf shot in the previous year's tournament. Agnew's tee shot veered into the gallery, hitting both an older man and his wife. The vice president quickly rushed to them to apologize, and then returned to the tee to hit another drive. His second drive was also wild and hit a woman in the ankle, which sent her to the hospital for x-rays.

President Ford had played in the Hope tournament many times, and hit a number of spectators in the process, including in 1995, while playing in the same group with sitting president Bill Clinton, former president Bush, Hope, and PGA Tour player Scott Hoch.

According to the *New York Times*, Ford yelled "Fore" as soon as he realized he'd hooked his drive, but it wasn't soon enough to help a woman who got struck in the finger by his ball.

#41 did some damage himself that day, eating a big piece of humble pie when, on the very first hole, his second shot bounced off a tree and bloodied a woman by hitting her in the nose and breaking her glasses. Later, on the fourteenth hole, his ball hit a man in the back of the leg.

But he birdied the sixth hole.

Back to Firestone, though, this time the president hit a pretty good drive. We walked down the fairway, with me toting his bag. He didn't hit a great second shot, but he advanced it pretty well as he is capable of doing. But the result was that he'd left his ball in the very worst position for his own ability: he was in four-inch deep, thick, Bluegrass rough. He had to play it out of that tangled rough and fly it over a bunker to an elevated green. He had to hit a flop shot high to accomplish that, and it's not a very comfortable shot for him (to be fair, it's a shot many amateur golfers are not comfortable with).

I handed him a club and gave him a little encouragement.

He stood over the ball, focused, took a swipe, and hit a perfect flop shot, landing the ball about two feet from the hole.

He and I looked at each other, both in shock it happened. Neither one of us wanted to say, "Good shot" or "Where'd that come from?" and break the magic of the moment. He nonchalantly took a putter and walked up to the green while I carried the bag around to the side of it. The crowd loved it.

On the second hole it was, as Yogi Berra once quipped, "déjà vu all over again," as the same scenario played out.

Later in the round we were on one of the tees, which is connected to another tee for another hole going the other direction. As we settled into our tee, we noticed Greg Norman was with his group on the other part of the tee. Norman brought his players over to meet the president and say hello. We chatted some and, of course, we had a couple of the Secret Service agents with us, one of whom was named Pete. I thought I'd tease Pete a little.

"Pete here is a 1-handicap," I told Norman. "He thinks he can outdrive you."

"Does he? Well, it's only a pro-am. Take your best shot and we'll see," Norman said, while handing Pete his driver and a ball.

"Oh, no, no," Pete, red-faced, said to Norman. "I know you hit the ball a long way!"

Everybody on the tee had a good laugh. But the Secret Service got revenge on me later in the round. The president had a towel on his golf bag he'd been given, and the snap on it that holds it to the bag had kind of worn out. So, while caddying, I'd dropped this towel along the way about three times. One of the agents would see this, pick it up, come over, and tap me on the shoulder and hand the towel to me.

The day went on, and we finished the round and went back to our bungalow where the tournament officials had organized a small, private event. It was a sit-down dinner with some sponsors of the tournament and Hale

Irwin. After that we went back over to the clubhouse for the president to shake some hands, accept his award, and say a few words. I was standing next to the president, so a lot of people mistook me for a Secret Service agent and would come over to me and ask permission to speak to the president.

At the end of the evening, about ten o'clock, we were about to leave to go fly back to Maine. We got on the airplane and taxied down the runway. As soon as we got into the air, one of the Secret Service agents approached President Bush.

"Sir," he said, "we just want to make you aware today that we had one situation on the golf course. We didn't bring it up to you earlier because we handled it without a problem."

That got the president's attention.

"What happened?" President Bush asked.

"Well, sir, it was your caddie. He dropped your towel three different times, creating a security problem. So we graded him."

He turned around and all the other agents were holding cards like the judges do during the skating or gymnastics competitions during the Olympics. They'd graded me 4.2, 6.8, and 5.1!

As he approached his mid-eighties, the president was struck with Parkinson's disease, which affects his mobility and his stability. That makes golfing very difficult for him. For a guy as active as he is, that was very hard for him to adjust to. But President Bush still has one thing he will always have: a tremendous amount of heart. He has passion for everything he does and the people he does it with. And in these latter years when he can't play golf, he still has that passion. He'll be out there in his golf cart watching us and cheering family and friends on, using all his fun golf lingo, just as if he were playing in the group—even though at this point he cannot.

During his many visits to Cape Arundel after becoming afflicted with Parkinson's, he would still chip and putt a bit or hit a shot here and there from the fairway and still exclaim, "I put a little feather on that one!" The spirit in his heart has never wavered.

On President Bush's eighty-sixth birthday, June 12, Jim Nantz had come out to be with him. They came out to the golf course along with Doro, the president's daughter, and the four of us set out on carts to play golf.

The aging president was energetic, but due to his vascular Parkinsonism, could no longer stand in balance to swing a golf club. Yet even though the president had spent his life being fiercely competitive in everything from tennis to horseshoes, he didn't seem bothered at all by riding around with us on his cart and not hitting golf shots. The president was, at least, out in the action—"playing" in his own way. He was ribbing Nantz for wayward putts. The president urged me to take the "Tiger line" and hit big, bold, daring drives. In between our shots President Bush, with Doro, was bombing around the course in his power cart as if it were a polo pony. For a guy who hadn't driven an automobile in decades, it was really his only opportunity to get behind the wheel and be independently mobile. It was similar to the freedom the president still had while at the helm of his beloved, dark blue offshore speedboat *Fidelity*. He'd power through the kick and the pitch and the wind and the waves with a determined glee. I'd always presumed that throttling up on that boat was the closest he could come to replicating his days in the Pacific during the Second World War as the US Navy's youngest aviator. Aboard *Fidelity* he'd scan the clouds over the horizon, check the radar, and ride the Atlantic waves as if they were turbulent updrafts.

Appearances on the golf course, though, or even on the backyard putting green at his family compound on Walker's Point, had become very rare since the president could no longer even use that long, Polecat putter he used to famously wield. Golf is in his blood, though, courtesy of Herbert Walker and Prescott Bush.

During the round, Nantz would, with his recognizable broadcast voice, launch into his "announcer speak" and call the action for fun: "*Ken Raynor . . . a club professional from Maine . . . not far from where Brad Faxon and Billy Andrade proved to PGA Tour fans that great golfers can, indeed, emerge from New England, now faces an approach shot demanding enough precision to give him the opportunity to do the same . . . and he'll attempt to prove it with the added pressure of the watchful eyes of the former leader of the free world upon him. . . .*"

We would laugh and learned, eventually, not to wait for Jimmy to finish one of his setup soliloquies before playing a shot—or the round would last well beyond the light-speed time in which the Bushes typically liked to finish playing.

We reached the sixth hole and paused for a moment to take in the scene and wave to a few passersby on the road.

"Mr. President," Nantz ventured, "ever had a hole-in-one here?"

"Nope," he answered. "Seen a lot. Never had one."

"Kenny?"

"I've had two, sir."

Jimmy let the topic go because he is intuitive and sensitive. But as he pulled a club from his bag, we both noticed the president peering at the green as he, himself, were sizing up which club he would use if he were able to play. Knowing President Bush's inherent optimism, I sensed it may also have surprised him to suddenly remember he'd never aced the little hole, though he had once come close.

Nantz broke the quiet with an idea: "Mr. President, would you like to take a shot?" Nantz then quickly explained himself. "Kenny and I can help you do it."

The president squinted at Nantz, and set his jaw. I walked over and stood next to Jim. I'd seen the look before. It wasn't a "no," but Nantz, a professional speaker, knew it was time to stay silent and not push the president.

"All right, let's give 'er a go," said President Bush from under his flat cap.

"One for the ages!" Nantz trumpeted. CBS's coverage of the PGA Championship each year always included the phrase: "Glory's Last Shot." And this would surely be one.

Without discussing it, Jimmy and I portrayed a nonchalant attitude and tone that this was all very normal procedure and no big deal. We wanted the president to feel as though he didn't really need us in order to hit the shot.

"What'll it be, Mr. President? 101 yards. Almost all carry. Slightly downhill. Not a breath of wind," Nantz intoned in his broadcast voice, but handed the president a wood before he could answer.

Nantz teed a ball for him and the president took a wide stance over it.

Doro grabbed a camera and started taking photos.

Because the president didn't have stability, I took a driver, stood behind him, and pointed the butt-end of the club, the handle, into the small of his back, with just enough pressure to let him feel I was there as backup to keep him from falling.

A lesser man might have been embarrassed by the effort — or unwilling to let his younger friends help him. But George Herbert Walker Bush never backed down from a challenge — politically or otherwise — and he relished the chance to give this hole, and his golf career, one last lash.

Glory would come to him in the mere striking of the ball. I could tell President Bush trusted Jimmy and me, so over this little golf shot he didn't seem unsteady or concerned about tumbling. The president, instead, was entirely focused and made his stroke.

He took a swing with the same intensity that sent his ball soaring down the first fairway of the Old Course at St. Andrews at the R&A Captain's Ceremony, a swing that once rocketed into the sky above Tiger Woods and the military members assembled at Congressional. That final golf shot of President Bush's life in the game was a peach that had him thrust his arms into the air in victory and high-five us while Doro documented it with the camera.

After all, no matter what game it is — the game of golf, the game of life, the game of grandfathering, you name it — the president is "all in."

11

I CALL HIM
"MR. PRESIDENT"

One Sunday afternoon, I was in casual conversation with Mrs. Bush at a quiet gathering on Walker's Point. We were watching one of the family's famous horseshoe pitching competitions at the narrow pits in between the house and the ocean. In between the clanging sound of the better-aimed horseshoes hitting the posts and the heckling heaped on anyone missing the mark, Mrs. Bush, speaking of her husband while watching him throw a horseshoe, asked, "Kenny, I'm curious. What do you call him?"

"Excuse me?" I asked.

She turned and looked up at me from under the shade of the brim of her big, pink gardening hat. "After all this time and all these years of friendship with George, what do you call him?"

I answered Bar sincerely and simply.

"I call him 'Mr. President.'"

Her head tilted as if to ask, "really?"

"We have such a warm relationship," I explained. "He's like my second dad. So, out of respect, I would not call my father by his first name either. It's not how I was raised. So, out of respect for my parents, and for President Bush, my 'second dad,' I don't call him 'George.'"

Mrs. Bush nodded with understanding for a moment and stared into my eyes, which likely had welled up with emotion.

The moment was snapped by the clang of a horseshoe and the sudden sound of the president yelling out, "Vic Damone!"—his trademark twist on the word "victory."

People query me with the same question Mrs. Bush did from time to time when they learn how much time I have spent playing golf, traveling, and fishing with my friend President Bush. And that's exactly what I call him: "President Bush." (Or some variation thereof, including "Sir.")

In a presidential situation or White House setting I call him "Mr. President."

In a social circumstance or appearance, especially with other people around, I might call him "Mr. Bush."

When I am referring to him while talking to other people, I call him "The President."

In the close proximity of fishing it's always "Mr. Bush," "Mr. President," or "Sir."

On the golf course, I might occasionally refer to him as "Partner."

Bar (never "Mrs. Bush" in this setting), then asked, "Has he ever said, 'Call me George?'"

"No, he has not. I think he knows I would not be comfortable with that."

I pinch myself that not only did I get to know the president, but that he took such an interest in knowing my family. I'll admit, though, that it wasn't just us. I can name an endless number of families who can say exactly what I am saying right now—how the president and Bar have reached out and shared these monumental life experiences.

There was one conversation that I had in 2016 that epitomizes my relationship with the president. Pulitzer Prize–winning author Jon Meacham came to play in the George H. W. Bush Celebrity Golf Classic that year. Meacham had just authored *Destiny and Power: The American Odyssey of George Herbert Walker Bush*, a giant, eight-hundred-page biography he'd written by listening, over the years, to the audio diaries of President Bush, which he recorded daily during his presidency and political career. We distributed the book to the participants in the tournament.

I found Meacham on the porch of Cape Arundel Golf Club in the morning, where he was about to give a live interview to Michael Patrick Shiels, who was hosting his syndicated show live from the tournament.

Before he went on the air, I approached Meacham to introduce myself.

"Thanks for coming, Mr. Meacham. I'm Ken Raynor, the head golf professional here at Cape Arundel Golf Club."

Meacham turned to me with a big smile.

"Of course I know who you are, Ken," he exclaimed. "Why, you're in President Bush's diaries as much as Gorbachev is!"

I was taken aback. Then Meacham continued, "He loves you very much."

Occasionally, President and Mrs. Bush have invited Anne and me to accompany them to an event that doesn't involve golf or the outdoors. Bar and the president attend, each year, a big fundraiser for the Barbara Bush Children's Hospital at Maine Medical Center. They've called us and asked us if we'd like to go with them to the Merrill Auditorium for the event. We'd first stop in Portland for dinner on the way.

The last few times we've gone, I've had the honor of pushing President Bush in his wheelchair through the side door for his grand entrance into the fundraiser. The theater was filled with a few thousand people supporting the children's hospital and hoping the Bushes would attend. It touched my heart when I pushed the wheelchair of the man I love and cherish into a standing ovation from a big crowd before the four of us took our seats.

We had such an active friendship fishing in rivers and playing speed golf. Now that President Bush is confined to a wheelchair, has it affected our relationship? That's a difficult question to answer, because it is an emotional one. I feel, in a sense, helpless because I would love to have those cherished moments back. I'm so happy that I lived each one of those active experiences with him to the fullest.

As for the president, his desire to still go do it is extremely high, but his body just won't let him.

"I wish we could go back up to the Tree River and fish again," President Bush said. I know how much he'd like to share those experiences again just as much as I'd like to do it with him, and it makes those times we did spend together even more special.

Bar says President Bush has never complained about his physical circumstances. He just keeps moving on, living life to the fullest, and focusing on the good. He never feels sorry for himself and doesn't want other people to either. President Bush enjoys the people that are around him and loves his family. He's lived an amazing, dynamic life — a life he's shared with all of us.

We almost lost him twice now in recent years. Both times it was in winter — and both times pneumonia put him in the intensive care unit at Houston Methodist Hospital for weeks.

The first was before Christmas in 2012. President Bush had been admitted in late November for the second time that month due to a stubborn cough. Eventually, though, he was placed in intensive care for bronchitis, which triggered complications, including a persistent fever. News reports did not look good for the eighty-eight-year-old former commander-in-chief.

It was tough because we didn't want to be in the way, but we cared deeply, as so many people did. The president's office did a very good job of keeping those close to him posted about his status with private emails.

The entire family typically comes to Boca Grande, Florida, at Christmastime, including the 43rd president, George W. Bush, who had been with his dad a day before he arrived. I met a tearful W. on the practice tee at Coral Creek Club. He told me he was unsure what would happen next. He said he'd almost felt like he was saying goodbye to his dad for the last time when he'd left the hospital in Houston.

I expressed to him our concerns and, because we've always been extremely sensitive about not encroaching personally, I was careful to ask how we could most appropriately send our best wishes his way without interrupting and being in the way of the family.

"Ken," said President George W. Bush, "you *are* family."

It was a very nice thing for him to say.

The news had been reporting a dramatic bedside vigil by his wife, children, grandchildren, and most members of his family, plus others, including James Baker III, his longtime friend who'd served as his secretary of state. President Bush though, in his typically self-deprecating manner, told his chief of staff Jean Becker to tell everyone to "put the harps back in the closet."

"Someday President Bush might realize how beloved he is, but of course one of the reasons why he is so beloved is because he has no idea," said Becker in a statement.

It took two months total, but the president emerged from the hospital in early 2013, and he even made it to parachuting in June of 2014 to celebrate his ninetieth birthday. By December of that year, though, he had another weeklong hospital stay, that time for shortness of breath.

Seven months later, in July of 2015, he fell at home at Walker's Point, broke a vertebra, and was in a neck brace for a while.

Between Christmas and New Year's 2016, President Bush and his extended family had their annual reunion at the historic Gasparilla Inn on Boca Grande Island. The genteel resort on the Gulf of Mexico has a Pete Dye–designed golf course, and it is very near the Coral Creek Club, a Tom Fazio–designed private club I helped develop and where I serve as head golf professional each winter. My son Kyle and I visited with the president and, about a week later, on January 6, he and Mrs. Bush, back in Houston, celebrated their seventy-second wedding anniversary.

Four days later, President Bush, who, like all former presidents, was invited to attend the inauguration events in Washington, DC on January 20, wrote a letter to President-Elect Donald Trump apologizing for not being able to attend:

> Barbara and I wish you the very best as you begin this incredible journey of leading our great country. My doctor says if I sit outside in January, it likely will put me six feet under. Same for Barbara. So I guess we're stuck in Texas.

Days after sending that letter, President Bush, without sitting outside in January, was nevertheless in Houston Methodist Hospital again with a persistent cough and pneumonia. As doctors intubated the ninety-two-year-old former president to keep his airway clear and assist with his breathing, Mrs. Bush, at age ninety-one, was admitted to the same hospital with fatigue, coughing, and likely bronchitis.

Mrs. Bush was out of her hospital bed after two nights, but the world held its breath until Jim Nantz, during the Patriots' NFL playoff game, finally announced on the air that President Bush had been moved out of the ICU. His spokesperson Jim McGrath confirmed that he was "on the upswing."

When he left the hospital over a week later, the relief was palpable.

None of us were ready to lose a close friend, a special person—and we never will be ready. President Bush, though, somewhere on a river or a golf course, broached the subject once with me.

"I am not afraid of death in any way shape or form," he insisted.

He loves life but he's a faithful man, so I get the sensation from him that he has a lot of faith. Faith can mean a lot of different things: faith in people and faith in God. He has both.

In his Inaugural Address on the West Front of the Capitol, President Bush said something that will forever remain in my memory because of its emphasis on using power to help people:

"[W]e are given power not to advance our own purposes, nor to make a great show in the world, nor a name. There is but one just use of power, and it is to serve people."

Sharing a quiet moment with beloved friend President George H. W. Bush at the home of friends Stephen and Alicia Spenlinhauer prior to the start of the Bush/ Pike Celebrity Golf Tournament. *(Photo by Robert Dennis)*

Epilogue

We all have mentors or very special occasions that reflect chapters in our lives that have had a huge impact and left lasting impressions. In this book I have shared a few in an effort to portray my incredible relationship with a man who will be remembered in our nation's history not only for his accomplishments but also for his passion for family, friends, and country.

These stories could go on and on, include many more people, and continue to portray the lust for life witnessed by all who have met Mr. Bush, but simply put, he has enriched all of our lives.

This book is not about me, which has been my largest concern during its writing, but I have many to thank for having been a part of it.

First and foremost, the Bush Family, from the Bush presidents and First Ladies, to Governor, Marvin, Neil, Doro, and their extended families. We have enjoyed years together not just on the golf course but at Walker's Point watching our families grow. Thank you to the respective staffs led by dear friend Jean Becker, who keeps her clubs by the door. And to the personal aides over the many years and all the support and trust of the Secret Service. To the incredible membership of Cape Arundel Golf Club, who have many of their own stories to share after their encounters with Golf Polo and Bush Golf, thank you!

It's these additional personal stories that are constantly shared by people that really tell the whole story and the value and impact that a moment in time meeting with the president can have.

I hope this book reminds us of all the good in living life to the fullest. If you did not know already, George Herbert Walker Bush has done just that!